Race Relations in Virginia
1870–1902

By

Charles E. Wynes

ROWMAN AND LITTLEFIELD
TOTOWA, N. J.
1971

Reprinted, 1971 by
Rowman and Littlefield

COPYRIGHT © 1961
BY
University of Virginia Press

ISBN 0-87471-013-8

Acknowledgments

THE cooperation and assistance of many individuals made this work possible. Indeed, without their aid it never would have been completed.

To Professor Edward Younger of the University of Virginia, who suggested the topic and then directed it through its many stages of creation and development, credit is due for this study's very existence. His example of scholarship was an inspiring one which the author sought to follow.

Professor Cecil Alan Hutchinson of the University of Virginia, and Professor Vernon Lane Wharton, Dean of the College of Liberal Arts at the University of Southwestern Louisiana, read the entire manuscript in its doctoral dissertation stage and made many valuable suggestions which were incorporated in the final version, to its great improvement.

Many other scholars likewise had a hand in its creation. Professor Lambert Molyneaux, of the Sociology Department of the University of Virginia, added greatly, through two of his courses, to the author's understanding of a problem which encompasses much more than history alone. Professor James H. Johnston, Dean; Professors James H. Brewer, Robert L. Clarke, and Harry Roberts, all of Virginia State College, made valuable bibliographical suggestions and were in general most helpful. Professor Roscoe Lewis of Hampton Institute readily gave up vacation time to consult with the author, make suggestions, and steer him to other helpful persons, such as Professor Philip S. Campbell, also of Hampton Institute, who made further bibliographical suggestions. Professor C. Vann Woodward of the Johns Hopkins University, read the M. A. thesis from which the study developed and graciously accepted the author's early criticisms of his *The Strange Career of Jim Crow*. Professor Bernard Mayo of the University of Virginia, Professor Allen W. Moger of Washington and Lee University, and Professor Raymond C. Dingledine, Jr., of Madison College, likewise read the master's thesis and offered suggestions incorporated in the present form. Mr. James A. Bear, Jr., now curator of Thomas Jefferson's Monticello, but formerly of the University of Virginia Library, offered invaluable insights into the history of post-Civil War Virginia and made available to the author his collection of the Thomas Staples Martin Politi-

iii

cal Papers. To Mr. John Cook Wyllie, Librarian of the University of Virginia, the author is indebted for more assistance, help, and advice of all kinds than he can enumerate here.

Invaluable over the years were the patience and assistance of numerous members of the Library Staff of the University of Virginia, especially Miss Roy Land, Miss Helena Koiner, Miss Mary Topping, Mrs. Mabel Talley, Miss Anne Freudenberg, Miss Katherine Beville, Mrs. George Davis, Mr. Francis L. Berkeley, and Mr. William H. Runge. The staffs of other libraries were equally helpful, especially Dr. Mattie Russell, Curator of Manuscripts, Duke University; also the staff of the Manuscripts Division of the Library of Congress, especially Mr. Russell Smith, formerly of the University of Virginia Library and equally helpful there; the staff of the Manuscripts Division of the University of North Carolina Library; Mrs. Robert L. Clarke of the Virginia State College Library; Miss Yvette Cameron of the Hampton Institute Library; and the entire staff of the Moorland Foundation, Howard University Library, but especially Mrs. Dorothy Porter, Supervisor.

Two regular-session grants-in-aid and one summer-session grant-in-aid from the Phelps-Stokes Fund at the University of Virginia, administered by Professor Floyd N. House, and later by Professor Edward Winter, helped underwrite the cost of research and travel involved in this study. Cost of publication was also borne by the Phelps-Stokes Fund.

I am indebted to Professor Joseph Milton Nance, Head of the Department of History at the Agricultural and Mechanical College of Texas, who very considerately kept my number of teaching preparations to a minimum so that I could devote more time to this work's completion.

For permission to cite material in the William Mahone Papers, Duke University Library, I am indebted to Mr. William M. McGill of Charlottesville and Mr. Henry P. McGill of Petersburg, Virginia, both of whom were most gracious and cooperative.

To Professor Joseph L. Blotner of the University of Virginia, who edited the manuscript for style, I am indebted for being saved from numerous pitfalls in syntax and expression. And to Mr. Charles E. Moran, Jr., Director of the University of Virginia Press, I am indebted for his patience, cooperation, and helpfulness, which ultimately brought this manuscript to the light of day.

And finally, I am indebted to my wife, Anna W. Wynes, who typed the manuscript through all of its many stages. She was ever a help and never an anchor in bringing this study to completion.

All of these persons are, however, absolved from responsibility for any controversial claims made in this work. They are my own, as is responsibility for any errors of fact.

Charles E. Wynes
The Agricultural and Mechanical
College of Texas

Preface

IN THE autumn of 1954, Professor C. Vann Woodward delivered the annual James W. Richard Lectures in History at the University of Virginia, subsequently published as *The Strange Career of Jim Crow* (New York, 1955). This book, which constitutes a milestone, albeit a controversial one, in the revisionist history of the South, is the basis of the study undertaken here. In this work, Professor Woodward makes no claim that a golden age in race relations ever existed in the South, but he maintains that the racial situation has not always been as dismal as most of us now living remember it prior to rejection of the "separate but equal" doctrine by the United States Supreme Court in 1954 (*Brown vs. Board of Education of Topeka*). He asserts, on the contrary, that the Negro was accorded during the Gilded Age a much higher place in Southern society than that he occupied during the early years of the twentieth-century.

Certain historical facts, also found in Woodward, should be stated before amplifying his thesis. In all of the Southern states, after Radical Reconstruction had ceased and therefore during the tenure of Redeemer or Bourbon governments, large numbers of Negroes once more or less freely voted. They also sent Negro members to local offices, state legislatures, and even to the national Congress. The segregation statutes, which have begun to fall so rapidly since 1954, do not date from Redemption in the 1870's, but rather from the late 1890's and early twentieth-century.

Professor Woodward flashes a light of scholarly skepticism into the too-often maligned and misunderstood era between the end of Radical Reconstruction and the 1890's. He contends that the segregation statutes achieved more than merely the legalizing of long-standing practices of segregation and ostracism. He maintains instead that the South, which has so long held that legislation cannot change its immutable folkways and mores, once had its racial customs and practices changed, or at least greatly altered, by the segregation statutes of the late nineteenth and early twentieth centuries. Black men, he says, did once ride side by side with white men on the railroads of the South (after the period of Republican, Carpetbag, Negro rule and during that of the native, white Redeemers) and they did, at least occasionally, meet white men in the same restau-

vii

rants, bars, and waiting rooms without benefit of even separating screens or partitions.

Professor Woodward's thesis is a bold and potentially powerful one put forward with reserve and moderation. It is also offered with an invitation to other scholars to look further into the comparatively unexplored recesses of race relations in the last thirty years of the nineteenth-century. Professor Woodward freely admits that subordination and exploitation were always present, even during Military and Radical Reconstruction, but he argues that ostracism and total segregation had to wait until the late 1890's and early twentieth-century. In his own words, his

> . . . only purpose has been to indicate that things have not always been the same in the South. In a time when Negroes formed a much larger proportion of the population than they did later, when slavery was a live memory in the minds of both races, and when the memory of the hardships and bitterness of Reconstruction was still fresh, the race policies accepted and pursued by the South were sometimes milder than they became later. The policies of proscription, segregation, and disfranchisement that are often described as the immutable 'folkways' of the South, impervious alike to legislative reform and armed intervention, are of a more recent origin. The effort to justify them as a consequence of Reconstruction and a necessity of the times is embarrassed by the fact that they did not originate in those times. And the belief that they are immutable and unchangeable is not supported by history. (p. 47)

And earlier, in the preface to *Jim Crow*, he says,

> Since I am . . . dealing with a period of the past that has not been adequately investigated . . . it is rather inevitable that I shall make some mistakes. I shall expect and hope to be corrected. In the meantime, I feel that the need of the times for whatever light the historian has to shed upon a perplexing and urgent problem justifies this somewhat premature effort. (p. ix)

The work which follows is an acceptance of the invitation to explore the Woodward thesis further, and to test its validity in the case of one specific Southern state. A final critical evaluation of it appears in the conclusion. The main body of the following study is also more generally a history of race relations in Virginia, 1870–1902. Thus, it is intended to be useful as more than just a selection of evidence relative to a particular thesis.

Table of Contents

Introduction

AFTER nine years of Civil War and Reconstruction, Virginia reentered the Union on January 26, 1870. On that date, President Grant signed into law a bill authorizing Virginia's restoration to the Union. Earlier, the Virginia General Assembly had ratified the Fourteenth and Fifteenth Amendments, as required for readmission. These amendments guaranteed to the Negro equal protection under the laws of the nation and provided that his right of suffrage should not be abridged because of race, color, or previous condition of servitude.

Thus thrust into society as a legal equal and onto the center of the political stage, the Virginia Negro was destined for the next thirty-one years to be the single most important factor in a turbulent period of social and political upheaval. His role was a significant one, from ratification of the liberal Underwood Constitution of 1868 down to and including approval of the constitutional convention which disfranchised him in 1902. Between these two events he was a decisive factor in the state debt readjustment controversy and in the development of a peculiar type of Virginia Populist party. His real significance in these events, however, lay more in his potential for action than in his actions themselves. His wishes were rarely consulted or heeded. Still his presence could never be ignored.

The position of the Negro in post-1870 Virginia was unique because Virginia reentered the Union firmly in the hands of native white Conservatives and moderate white Republicans. This conservative political leadership had brought about reentry sooner than might otherwise have been possible primarily through shrewd political bargaining with the federal government. The realistic, white, Virginia Conservatives and moderate, white Republicans together had obtained from the Congress and President Grant a chance for the state to vote separately on the general body of the new constitution and on two provisions contained in it.

One of the provisions of the new constitution would have deprived of the right of suffrage all persons who had ever held any public office in which an oath of allegiance to the United States was required, and who had subsequently engaged in rebellion or insurrection against the United States, or given aid and comfort to those so engaged. The other provision would have barred from public office all persons who could not take the so called "iron clad" or "test oath" that they had never held office in the Confederacy or in any way given it aid, support, or comfort. The first provision would have disfranchised Virginia's elite, its white leadership—a humiliating blow to their pride and to the state's pride. The second provision would have barred from public office the overwhelming majority of white Virginians. Thus the only white Virginians who could have held public office had this provision been accepted, would have been those who, from genuine Union principles of conscience or conviction had not supported the Confederacy, newcomers to the state since the war, and those who lacked either the convictions or the courage actively to support either side during the war.

A vote on a constitution containing these provisions would have rejected it. But given a chance to vote separately on these provisions aside from the general body of the constitution, a majority of white Virginians were willing to accept Negro suffrage and other liberal provisions which they regarded as radical.

The Underwood Constitution which contained these obnoxious provisions was completed on April 17, 1868, but not until July 6, 1869, was it submitted to a public vote. Hostility to the disfranchising and test oath provisions had continued to grow during all this time, so that whereas Republican leaders had at first been afraid to submit the constitution to the electorate, they later became afraid to withhold it longer, as they saw hostility toward it rapidly increasing.

The first public inkling that there might be a way out of the dilemma of either accepting a humiliating constitution or continuing under Military Reconstruction came in a letter signed *Senex*, which appeared in the Richmond *Whig* and Richmond *Dispatch* on December 28, 1868. Its author was Alexander H. H. Stuart, former Whig congressman from western Virginia, Secretary of the Interior under Fillmore, and an opponent of secession. Stuart, a devoted friend of Henry Clay, from whom he apparently learned well the value of compromise, proposed that Virginia gracefully yield on the point of Negro suffrage in return for the opportunity to vote separately on the question of Confederate proscription. Immediate reaction to the proposal was one of bitter opposition, but there were many who saw the wisdom of the proposal. Among these were moderate Virginia Republicans who opposed their more radical brethren.

Under Stuart's leadership a Committee of Nine was formed to go to Washington and bargain for the opportunity to vote separately on the proscription provisions in return for acquiesence on the question of Negro suffrage. The Committee of Nine was aided before Congress by a delegation of moderate Republicans from Virginia and opposed by a delegation of radical Republicans. The issue was decided when, on April 7, 1869, President Grant recommended to Congress that Virginia be authorized to vote separately on the general body of the constitution and on the proscription provisions. On April 10, Congress empowered the President to call an election in Virginia on those terms.

Meanwhile the split in Virginia's Republican party had become apparent. Virginia had always had a thoroughly respectable political group holding Whiggish or Republican principles whose members now came to oppose the views of radicals in their party. The radicals were led by Governor Henry Wells and counted among their followers most of the Negroes, as well as many white newcomers to the state. In May, 1868, before the Stuart compromise was proposed, Wells had been nominated for governor under the new constitution. Largely as a result of Wells' radical views, which split the state Republican party, the state committee met in January, 1869, and set aside the nomination, calling for a new convention in March. Wells, who was on intimate terms with officials of the Baltimore and Ohio Railroad, had gained the distrust and opposition of General William Mahone, who had his own designs for railroad consolidation in Virginia. Wells' accession to the governor's office with the approval and backing of outside railroad interests might have hindered both the economic and political plans of the ambitious little Billy Mahone.

The Wells forces were in control of the March convention and succeeded in nominating him again. A colored delegate, however, nominated Dr. J. D. Harris, a Negro, for lieutenant governor. This constituted political suicide, and Edgar Allen, a Mahone follower, quickly seized the opportunity presented to discredit the Wells ticket completely. In a speech that blinded the Negro delegates to political reality, Allen seconded Harris' nomination, and the convention named him for second place on the ticket. Moderate Republican voters now faced a dilemma. Under the leadership of Mahone, Edgar Allen, and George Rye—a devious and mysterious individual from the Valley but a native of the state of Maryland—the moderate Republicans tried for a solution by nominating Gilbert Carleton Walker, a little known but able and moderate carpetbagger. To gain the backing of both Unionists and Valley Republicans, they nominated John T. Lewis, a Union supporter from Rockingham county in the Valley for lieutenant governor.

The white Conservatives of Virginia had meanwhile nominated a ticket headed by Robert E. Withers. Their position was one of uncompromising opposition to the Underwood Constitution in its entirety, in which they probably had the backing of most white Virginians. Opposed to the Withers group were the radical Republicans headed by Governor Henry Wells, who had the backing of nearly all the Negroes and a majority of the white Republicans. They approved of the Underwood Constitution, including the Confederate proscription clauses. With these two groups the issues were clear cut—the Underwood Constitution or not, just as it stood. Complicating this picture were the compromisers—realistic Conservatives and moderate or true Republicans, as they called themselves, headed by Gilbert C. Walker. This faction approved the body of the Underwood Constitution, minus the proscription clauses.

Lacking a majority of even the white Republican voters, the moderate Republicans saw that their only hope lay in getting the Conservatives to withdraw their ticket and back Walker instead. The Conservatives, fearing the more concentrated and entrenched Wells forces and also suspecting that Wells might be counted in as governor even if he lost, were induced by Mahone and the Committee of Nine, led particularly by John B. Baldwin, to settle for half a loaf and accept Negro suffrage, by withdrawing their candidate and backing Walker.

With only two tickets in the race now, both headed by carpetbaggers, the issue became largely one of blacks *vs.* whites. Some few Negroes came over to the moderate Republicans, but most white Virginians who voted for Walker did so because it was the only way they could vote against the body of Negroes and the white radicals allied with them. They did not vote for Negro suffrage. They voted to *accept* it, because the alternative appeared to be Negro rule under the leadership of radical Republicans.

The fusion of Conservatives with moderate Republicans resulted

Introduction

in Walker's defeating Wells by a vote of 119,535 to 101,204, on July 6, 1869. The body of the constitution was approved, while the disfranchising article was defeated by a vote of 124,360 to 84,410, and the "test oath" measure by a vote of 124,715 to 83,458.[1]

By this vote Virginia had been saved from all real possibility of Negro rule, although the cry of "Negro rule" was to serve as an inflammatory, political shibboleth to be bandied about in nearly every election for the next thirty-one years. Though these facts have been long known to scholars, they have been too frequently overlooked in telling the story of Virginia's turbulent history between 1870 and 1902. Taken together with the rise of the liberal but dictatorial William Mahone (long before the other Southern states produced their own liberal reformers), they serve to explain in large measure much that happened in Virginia before 1902 which made her "different" from her sister Confederate states. Even more, they serve to make the story of the Virginia Negro and race relations "different"— a fact commented on by many observers from outside the state.

Still the Virginia Negro in 1870 was hopeful, optimistic, and confident. Never had his future been so bright. Soon, however, he became discouraged and despondent, belligerent and disillusioned with the Republican party, as he realized how complete had been the triumph of white Conservatives and moderate Republicans. From 1879–1883 his hopes were again raised and his future brightened as the Readjusters, under the leadership of Mahone, accorded him the greatest measure of justice and liberal reform that had yet been his lot. But even then the Promised Land was not at hand, for after 1883 the Negro was inexorably shunted aside, deprived of political privilege, and put "in his place," as the way was paved for his disfranchisement in 1902.

---

[1] Hamilton James Eckenrode, "History of Virginia Since 1865: 1865–1945— A Political History" (Unpublished manuscript in the University of Virginia Library), 50 ff.

Chapter 1

The Conservative Triumph, 1869-1878

IN THE election of July 6, 1869, which made Gilbert C. Walker governor, 180 members of the new General Assembly were also elected. They included twenty-seven Negro members—six in the Senate of forty-three members, and twenty-one in the House of Delegates of 137 members. In the Senate there were thirty Conservatives and thirteen Republicans, while in the House the proportion was ninety-five Conservatives (three Negroes) to forty-two Republicans. Thus in both houses the native white Conservatives had a clear majority.[1]

This fact raises the interesting speculation of whether the Conservatives might not have been able to elect their own gubernatorial candidate, Robert E. Withers. In withdrawing Withers in favor of the compromise, moderate Republican, Walker, they may have acted overcautiously. Election of Withers could have produced an administration markedly different from that which developed under Walker, particularly with regard to the state's railroad interests, in the disposal of which, Walker was instrumental. Speculation from this point could run riot, because retention of the railroad investments might have prevented development of the conditions which gave rise to the Readjuster party and William Mahone. And without Mahone, the story of the years 1870–1902, would be completely different.

With the Conservatives in control in 1870–1871 and with the Republican party split into a moderate and a radical group, it is not surprising that the English traveler, Robert Somers, found the tone of Virginia politics to be moderate. Comparing politics in New York and Virginia, he found those of Virginia to be the more temperate.[2] In the House of Delegates, Somers noted how the three or four Negro members whom he saw mingled freely with the white delegates—probably white Republican delegates, however. But in the Senate,

---

[1] William C. Pendleton, *Political History of Appalachian Virginia, 1776–1927* (Dayton, Virginia, 1927), 294.

[2] Robert Somers, *The Southern States Since the War, 1870–71* (London and New York, 1871), 16.

the two Negro members whom he saw kept apart from the white senators. "Yet they seemed to take a cordial interest in the proceedings, and manifested all sympathy with the Senators who addressed the House [*i.e.* the Senate]." ³

In forty of Virginia's ninety-nine counties in 1870 Negroes outnumbered the white population, and where this was so, outward appearances were often not so amicable as in the state capital of Richmond. Particularly in cities such as Petersburg, Norfolk, and Danville, where there were large Negro populations, friction, ill feeling, and rivalry were apparent. In 1871, a Petersburg correspondent wrote to the editor of the Richmond *Daily Dispatch:*

> There is considerable feeling here that the Legislature should do something for the relief of Petersburg from the yoke of Radical and negro rule which rides her bowed neck. The burthen becomes heavier and more oppresive every day.⁴

In 1873–1874, Edward King of *Scribners' Monthly* magazine observed:

> There is a large negro population in Norfolk, and the white citizens make great struggles at each election to keep the municipal power in their own hands.⁵

Though few areas of the state were ever in such danger, the Conservative-controlled legislature in 1871 heeded the plea for salvation from Negro domination by gerrymandering several counties. Altering their borders, the legislature broke up black majorities. Under the guise of congressional reapportionment, political boundaries were successively redrawn in 1874, 1876, 1878, 1883, and 1891, by the Conservatives or Democrats, always to the detriment of the Negro voter.⁶ The 1869–1870 session of the General Assembly also passed a law requiring that lists of qualified voters be kept separate according to race of black or white.⁷ This created an almost infinite

---

³ *Ibid.*, 17.
⁴ Richmond *Daily Dispatch*, August 28, 1871.
⁵ Edward King, *The Great South* (Hartford, Connecticut, 1875), 592.
⁶ Robert E. Martin, "Negro Disfranchisement in Virginia," in vol. I of *The Howard University Studies in the Social Sciences* (Washington, D. C., 1938), 84; Paul Lewinson, *Race, Class, and Party: A History of Negro Suffrage and White Politics in the South* (London, New York, and Toronto, 1932), 65.
⁷ *Acts of the General Assembly of the State of Virginia, 1869–1870*, p. 56.

number of opportunities for chicanery, not the least of which was the ease of "losing" the list of colored voters.

Strangely, however, in this situation it was hard to separate fact from fiction in racial feeling, or to match the railings of conservative newspaper editors with what were often amiable relations between the races on political matters. At the Conservative party convention of August 30, 1871, where the party was reorganized to the extent that the old "traditional Virginia leadership" began once more to pick up the reins of power, six Negro delegates from Richmond were welcomed and seated.[8] At a Conservative political meeting in Amelia county on November 2, just before the 1871 election was held, white and black sat together on the stage and both gave speeches.[9] Still, the election was decided on the basis of the race question, with almost all whites voting Conservative and an equal proportion of the Negroes voting Republican.[10] Such political divisions were fostered in considerable measure by editorials like the following:

> [The Republican party of Virginia] consists of negroes who are utterly incompetent to exercise intelligibly [*sic*] any political right, and who are utterly incapable of filling any responsible office.[11]

Confusion, prejudice, and race chauvinism were indeed abroad in the land.

The Virginia Republican party had split over the character and views of Governor H. H. Wells and the election of Gilbert C. Walker as the new governor. That fact alone made it apparent to the Negro that he could not always count upon the Grand Old Party for support. This loss was further aggravated by an even more uncomfortable fact which rapidly became increasingly apparent: white, radical Republicans were using the Negro to keep themselves in political office while they showed little real desire for justice for the Negro, and were often as willing to exploit him as they were to exploit the native whites. It was a fact that white, radical Republicans controlled their wing of the party and usually nominated white candidates —and Negro Republicans were quick to point it out. The Conserva-

---

[8] Richard L. Morton, *The Negro in Virginia Politics, 1865–1902* (Charlottesville, Virginia, 1919), 84.
[9] Richmond *Daily Dispatch*, November 6, 1871.
[10] Eckenrode, "History of Virginia Since 1865," p. 86.
[11] Richmond *Daily Dispatch*, September 15, 1871.

tives exploited the advantage this gave them by constantly working to widen the alienation of Negro Republican leadership from white Republican leadership.[12]

A typical example of tactics the Negro Republicans condemned occurred at an 1871 radical Republican nominating convention, which met in Richmond to nominate candidates for the state Senate from Henrico county and the city of Richmond, and candidates for the House of Delegates from the city of Richmond only. Nominations for the Senate went off well and impartially enough. J. H. Shields, white, and the Reverend William Troy, colored, received the Senate nominations, easily beating out two other candidates—both white. But there was no such harmony in choosing nominees for the House. Only twelve men were present, about equally divided between the two races, but five white candidates were nominated, and no Negroes. Lewis Lindsey, colored, objected to the all-white slate and stated that he could not go back to his constituents and tell them that the African race had again been slighted. A colored man named Forrester attempted to restore harmony by stating that he desired only a ticket that would win and adding that he saw the five nominated as making such a ticket. A white man named Burgess then brought forth the old weapon that "to place a colored man on the ticket would be to risk the success of the party." Landon Boyd, another colored delegate, passionately declared that "the negroes were getting tired of voting for white men only, and being told to wait," but the white ticket prevailed.[13] Later, the Executive Committee of the state Republican party declared the House nominations to be null and void and called a meeting for October 7 to further consider the dispute.[14] When a new slate of candidates was nominated, it still contained not a single colored candidate.[15]

It was not surprising that in the election of November, 1871, Negro representation in the General Assembly was reduced. The Conservatives in control were constantly growing stronger, and the Republicans split into moderates and radicals, with neither Republican

---

[12] Martin, "Negro Disfranchisement in Virginia," *Howard University Studies in the Social Sciences*, I, p. 88; Alrutheus A. Taylor, "The Negro in the Reconstruction of Virginia," *The Journal of Negro History*, XI (April and July, 1926), 525–526; also available in book form under the same title and published in Washington, D. C., 1926.

[13] Richmond *Daily Dispatch*, September 25, 1871.

[14] *Ibid.*, October 5, 1871.

[15] *Ibid.*, October 9, 1871.

group being overly friendly to the idea of Negro officeholders. From twenty-one Negro members in the House, the number was reduced to fourteen. In the Senate, Negro membership was halved, from six to three. Meanwhile the Conservatives increased their majority in the House by fifteen and in the Senate by six.[16] The attrition of every election steadily reduced Negro membership in the General Assembly, till finally, in 1891, the Negro no longer sat in the nation's oldest, representative, legislative assembly. By that date, many more members of the African race were qualified to participate in state lawmaking, just as thousands more were better qualified to vote than had been the case in 1869. But while the Negro had been improving himself to play a significant role in a democracy, white conservatives had also vastly improved old devices and devised new techniques for assuring white supremacy and keeping the Negro in his place, which did not include the legislative halls or even the polling booths.

From the moment party lines were drawn in post-Civil War Virginia, the Conservatives constituted the anti-Negro party just as the Republican party had already come to be identified as the pro-Negro party. The Conservative party, a motley group of old-line Democrats, Liberal Republicans, and former Whigs who refused to identify themselves with Northern Republicanism, was held together by the race issue.[17]

In the elections of 1869 and 1871, the keynote of the Conservative campaign had been the race issue, but at neither time was the color line drawn. Many Negroes had therefore voted with the coalition of Conservatives and moderate Republicans. But in the election of 1873, the Conservatives drew the racial line and called on the whites to be true to their color.[18] From that point on, Negroes were driven into Republican party ranks [19] where, admittedly, most of them would probably have gone by choice. One cannot avoid the conclusion, however, that by taking a thoroughly anti-Negro stand, the Conservatives, and later the Democrats, were as guilty as the Negroes in bringing about the situation where issues in a campaign always had to take a backseat to race loyalty.

---

[16] Nelson Morehouse Blake, *William Mahone of Virginia: Soldier and Political Insurgent* (Richmond, Virginia, 1935), 137.

[17] Eckenrode, "History of Virginia Since 1865," p. 88.

[18] Pendleton, *History of Appalachian Virginia*, 312–313.

[19] Taylor, "Negro in the Reconstruction of Virginia," *Journal of Negro History*, XI, pp. 515–516.

In 1873, the Conservatives for the first time felt themselves strong enough to stake the whole campaign on the race issue. Had they believed it a safe course, they would undoubtedly have done so earlier. Offering a liberal platform and pledging justice and education for both races, the Conservatives took to the stump holding up the "horrible example of Negro and white Radical rule" in other Southern states and alleging that same rule to be the case in certain Virginia localities.[20] Rightly confident that the world was going their way, they refused to settle upon a moderate Republican as a compromise gubernatorial candidate and offered their own General James L. Kemper, a veteran of Pickett's charge, wounded and captured at the battle of Gettysburg. A native of Madison county in the Piedmont, Kemper enjoyed the confidence of William Mahone— a signal blessing for any Virginia office-seeker at that date.

The views of the Richmond *Daily Dispatch* were typical of the tenor in which the Conservative campaign was waged. On March 4, 1873, the *Dispatch* asked, "Shall the whites rule and take care of the negroes, or shall the negroes rule and take care of the whites?" The issue thus stated and oversimplified in a wholly unrealistic manner, there was little doubt as to what the average white man's reply would be. Coming somewhat nearer the truth, while still making real political hay, the *Dispatch* also declared:

> . . . the Conservative party is the white man's party, and the Radical party is the negro party. The former proposes to keep all the offices in the hands of the whites, and the latter is *forced* to divide the offices with the negroes.[21]

The Staunton *Spectator*, speaking from a Conservative stronghold in the Valley, added explanation and warning:

> In self-protection, without any desire to injure the negroes, the whites are forced to unite and vote against the blacks, who if successful, will make Virginia another South Carolina [and] bring upon the State . . . mixed churches, mixed hotels, and mixed places of amusements.[22]

In Augusta county, of which Staunton was the county seat, the Negro population was less than twenty percent of the total, while in

20 *Ibid.*, 517; Morton, *Negro in Virginia Politics*, 89.
21 Richmond *Daily Dispatch*, April 28, 1873.
22 Staunton *Spectator*, September 9, 1873.

neighboring Highland county, there were only sixty-nine registered Negro voters in 1873.[23]

The state elections of 1873 marked with finality the end of all threat of Radical rule in Virginia. Conservative reaction and retrenchment went on apace until the more liberal-minded members of the Conservative party revolted, largely over the question of the state debt, and formed the Readjuster party.

A typical reaction to the Conservative victory of 1873 was expressed in a letter of congratulation to Governor-elect Kemper:

> Allow me to congratulate you . . . upon your elevation to the highest office in the state . . . and I also congratulate the Conservative party of the Old Dominion upon their selection [of] you . . . in their recent struggle to preserve and perpetuate the white man's ascendancy in our beloved 'Old Commonwealth.' It will have a happy influence upon the poor negroes. Many of them will see in their late overwhelming defeat, that they have been markedly deceived by the infamous Carpet Baggers [sic] & Scalawags and will learn, that their true policy is to harmonize and act with their old masters, more than they have heretofore done.[24]

The depression beginning in 1873 and the general turning away from the Republican party in 1874 following exposure of the Grant scandals left the South to do with the Negro as it would, because the North then turned to its own fiscal and moral problems.[25] Idealism, born of wartime patriotism and nurtured by postwar prosperity, had grown weak indeed by 1873. Both morally and financially, charity was now needed at home, and the Southern Negro was left to fend for himself.

Virginia Conservatives were not slow to seize the opportunity presented for tightening their own control at the expense of the Negro. As a result of the election of 1873, Conservatives outnumbered Republicans by at least three-to-one in both houses of the General Assembly. In the House of Delegates there were ninety-nine Conservatives to thirty-three Republicans, and in the Senate there were thirty-three Conservatives to nine Republicans.[26] The people already had before them a proposed amendment to abolish a third of the

---

[23] *Ibid.*, November 4, 1873.
[24] William H. Terrell to James L. Kemper, November 7, 1873. James L. Kemper Papers (University of Virginia Library).
[25] Morton, *Negro in Virginia Politics*, 88–89.
[26] *Ibid.*, 89.

local offices of the state. They promptly endorsed it, and the new legislature further proposed a whole series of amendments to the Underwood Constitution. The first of these added *petit* larceny to the recognized disqualifications from voting, which already included insanity, bribery at elections, embezzlement of public funds, dueling, treason, and all felonious crimes. This amendment was aimed at the Negroes, of course, whose lower element seemed to be peculiarly addicted to chicken-stealing. No one, however, was so fatuous as to claim that the proposed amendment was designed to discourage petty theft or to protect white Virginians' poultry.

Other amendments proposed included reduction of the House of Delegates' membership from 137 to 100, power for the General Assembly to provide for the government of cities and towns, power for the General Assembly to remove voting disqualifications incurred through dueling participation, and payment of a poll tax as a prerequisite to voting.[27] Reduction of the number of Delegates in the House would serve to further remove the government from the hands of the people and to pave the way for breaking up Negro enclaves through reapportionment by gerrymander. The proposal to empower the legislature to determine the form of government for cities and towns would break up Negro control in local areas. The poll tax payment amendment, in spite of all the propaganda that it was designed to insure revenue for public school support, was clearly aimed at the poorer Negroes who might not vote if they had to pay for the privilege. Such propaganda appeared to be all the more valid in light of the fact that Public School Superintendent William H. Ruffner proposed as early as 1873 that the poll tax revenue, earmarked by law for public school use, be doubled to two dollars and its payment made a prerequisite to voting.[28]

In 1876, all of these amendments were ratified by a large majority, with Conservatives generally approving them and Republicans opposing them.[29] Thus by legal and illegal means, those in political office were paying heed to their constituents who demanded a limited suffrage, chiefly at the expense of the Negro. Said a constituent of Congressman John Randolph Tucker in 1875: "I think we ought to

---

[27] *Ibid.*, 91–92.
[28] Tipton Ray Snavely, *The Taxation of Negroes in Virginia* (Phelps-Stokes Fellowship Paper of the University of Virginia, 1916), 15–16.
[29] *Appleton's Annual Cyclopaedia* (1876), 800.

aim, vigorously, for ultimate *limited suffrage*—at all hazards." [30] The poll-tax amendment of 1876 was, in part, an answer to that plea. The years 1869–1878 belonged to the Conservatives. In power from the beginning, they constantly tightened their hold on the state and successfully worked for the destruction of the Republican party and the removal of the Negro as an important political factor. While neither aim was achieved completely, after 1873, it was safe to let another issue—the state debt—replace that of the Negro as the foremost question to be dealt with. And by 1878, "the Republican party in Virginia had become a nullity." In 1877, it had not even offered a gubernatorial candidate. On the eve of the Readjuster period, one-party rule and white supremacy were near accomplished facts in Virginia. [31]

Driven from the polls by intimidation in the forms of violence and economic reprisal, and by legal measures such as the poll tax and disfranchisement for conviction of petty theft, the Virginia Negro by the end of the 1870's was in despair. Insult was added to political injury by the closing of many of his schools for lack of money to operate them. How then was he even to equip himself for participation in a democratic government? His own political party, as it sank toward oblivion in Virginia, deserted him, and worse yet, increasingly resorted to using him. No wonder Negro Republican leaders, meeting in Richmond in 1875, called on the national Republican party for aid—but in vain. They declared to their erstwhile Northern allies that they were suffering

> at the hands not only of the white citizens and local government of Virginia, but also at the hands of the leaders of the Republican party within the State and in the Federal capital. [32]

The Negro newspaper, *Virginia Star*, sadly commented on the Conservative legislature of 1878, which with

> the treasury bankrupt, the credit of the State grievously impaired, the schools closed or running on crutches . . . forgetting or neglecting

---

[30] O. Gray to John Randolph Tucker, August 16, 1875. Tucker Family Papers, Southern Historical Collection (University of North Carolina Library).

[31] Taylor, "Negro in the Reconstruction of Virginia," *Journal of Negro History,* XI (1926), 518; Eckenrode, "History of Virginia Since 1865," p. 94; Martin, "Negro Disfranchisement in Virginia," *Howard University Studies in the Social Sciences,* I, p. 89; Morton, *Negro in Virginia Politics,* 96.

[32] Martin, "Negro Disfranchisement in Virginia," *Howard University Studies in the Social Sciences,* I, pp. 87–88.

their duty to the people . . . [was] wasting time and money in trying to defeat the rights and liberties of colored citizens. . . .

The legislature at this time was discussing the "mode and measure of redress" against Judge Alexander Rives for the "usurpation" of requiring that Negroes be placed on juries trying Negro offenders before his court.[33]

Not only was the Virginia Negro restive, so were vast numbers of white Virginians from both major political parties. White and black were caught in the economic vise of the 1873–1879 depression. The "principle of Virginia honor," which had demanded in 1871 that the state's prewar indebtedness be paid in full, did not seem nearly so demanding and sacred by the late 1870's. And once again, by 1879, the old sectional differences and imbalance between East and West had boiled up anew and the West was demanding redress as it had first done in 1676, and repeated in 1812, 1829, 1831–1832, and more recently and disastrously, in 1861.

Economically and politically the stage was set for the emergence of new leaders—liberal, progressive, realistic, but cost-conscious men, unmarried to the past and hoary tradition. The Conservative party had itself largely brought on the conditions which nearly destroyed it. That a leader such as William Mahone should seize the reins of popular discontent and widely exploit it should not have surprised anyone. For the ensuing years from 1879 through 1883, Virginia would be consumed by the questions of the state debt, progressive reform, and heavy-handed political autocracy—all emanating from the dyspeptic little "Hero of the Crater," General William Mahone.

---

[33] Richmond *Virginia Star*, December 14, 1878.

Chapter 2

Political Revolution, 1879–1883

ONLY deep discontent on the part of the people could have brought about such a change in government as took place in Virginia in the state elections of 1879. The representatives of Virginia's "best people"—the Conservatives who by fusion with moderate Republicans had "redeemed" the state as it returned to the Union and then "saved it from Negro rule"—were abruptly swept from power in both houses of the legislature. A new group of leaders whose political careers began only after 1870 were brought in, men who were usually lacking in the ancestry and tradition so characteristic of earlier Virginia leadership. These men were liberals and realists in a Virginia of entrenched conservatism. Many of them were also opportunists, and some were even erratic visionaries given to supporting any minority cause. Among the latter was Mahone's later compatriot in the U. S. Senate, Harrison Holt Riddleberger, who championed lost causes including that of the Irish *Clanna Gael*. The Readjusters, as this new leadership was known, gained in the election of 1879 a total of fifty-six of the one-hundred Delegates' seats and twenty-four of the forty Senate seats. Eleven Negro members were elected to the House and two to the Senate.[1] The primary issue among those which made this victory possible was that of the state debt and the question of its full payment or readjustment.

By the end of the Civil War Virginia's pre-war indebtedness, plus unpaid interest accumulated during the war, had mounted to about forty million dollars. This debt had been incurred by the state's sponsoring internal improvements which, had the war not occurred, would have represented good investments. But after the war full payment of the debt with interest meant financial ruin for Virginia. The legislature had pledged payment of the debt in full in March, 1866, but Military Reconstruction intervened; and by the date of Virginia's readmission to the Union, debt and interest amounted to forty-six million dollars. Zealously guarding the state's honor, the Conservative legislature pushed through the Funding Act of 1871.

---

[1] Blake, *William Mahone*, 182.

This act issued new bonds paying six percent interest in return for two-thirds the amount of the old bonds plus interest. For the remaining third—West Virginia's share—interest-bearing certificates were issued whose payment was to be in accordance with future settlement with the state of West Virginia. Preceding passage of the Funding Act, Virginia had begun disposing of its railroad holdings, which were the major source of the debt but which, could have been a major source of revenue. Following passage of this act, revenues of the state did not prove sufficient to meet both the interest payments on the debt and normal state operating expenses, now greatly increased by the cost of the public school system. Furthermore, incoming revenue was reduced because interest coupons were receivable in payment of taxes. As a result, school funds were soon drawn upon to meet other expenses and make interest payments. The state then became divided into Funders and Readjusters—*i. e.*, those who wanted to pay the debt in full and those who wanted to scale it down.

Public opinion became so divided and inflamed over this issue and the general economic and financial condition of the state that there ceased to be a united front against the Negro. The Negroes naturally tended to side with the Readjusters, because most of the debt stemmed from expenditures made during antebellum days, and they stood to gain nothing from its payment. They felt that money spent on the debt should be used for schools, instead of school-fund money's being diverted to other purposes till some schools had to be closed for lack of operating funds.

The white farmers also opposed the debt-paying, conservative-lawyer legislators because they felt that they were being burdened with taxation to pay a debt to the lawyer-legislators' clients, the bondholders and syndicates. Thus, in the white farmers' eyes, many Virginia legislators were held to be guilty of economic oppression motivated by professional identification and association even if this was not always the actual fact.[2]

The battle between Funders and Readjusters was also a contest

---

[2] Taylor, "Negro in The Reconstruction of Virginia," *Journal of Negro History*, XI (1926), 518–519; Beverley B. Munford, *Random Recollections* (New York, 1905), 144. For the debt question, see Charles C. Pearson, *The Readjuster Movement in Virginia* (New Haven, Conn. and London, 1917); Richard L. Morton, *History of Virginia—Virginia Since 1861* (Chicago and New York, 1924); Elizabeth H. Hancock, editor, *Autobiography of John E. Massey* (New York and Washington, 1909).

between sections and classes or, in the eyes of many, between sections and castes. Those in favor of paying the debt represented the existing order, and their officeholders consisted largely of men from eastern and central Virginia. Thus the battle was a continuation of the old East *vs.* West conflict, long characteristic of the state.[3] With respect to class, the Readjuster movement "cut across racial lines and assumed the more fundamental aspects of a realistic political alignment having economic interest as its reason for existence." [4] This alignment of Negroes, small farmers, and those of modest means, against the "Bourbon Aristocrats," represented the first political alignment along class lines since the war.[5]

There was also an element of idealistic hope in the establishment of the Readjuster party: the hope that genuine two-party politics could be developed in Virginia.

> . . . the readjustment of the state debt was the issue given forth to the public, but the real design and effort was to bring about in Virginia a real two-party state.[6]

Analyzing the election results a few months later, the Negro newspaper, *Virginia Star*, editorialized:

> Gen. Mahone [leader of the Readjusters] was shrewd enough to see that since the war there had grown up generations of citizens who felt no enthusiasm for the old shibboleths, and he owes his political strength, in a considerable degree, to the support he has received from this class.[7]

Mahone and the Readjusters also gained by Conservative loss of strength and face through evidence of corruption. In one instance of it, the Conservative state treasurer was indicted in 1873 for defalcation and embezzlement but escaped trial by pleading insanity; in 1877, more embezzlement came to light in the form of canceled bonds which had been illegally refunded and added to the state debt. As Professor Woodward writes, "These revelations did not strengthen the Funders' case for sacrificing the public schools to the

[3] Munford, *Random Recollections*, 143.

[4] George W. Crawford, "John Mercer Langston—A Study in Virginia Politics," M. A. Thesis, Virginia State College (Petersburg, Virginia, 1940), 29.

[5] Martin, "Negro Disfranchisement in Virginia," *Howard University Studies in the Social Sciences*, I, p. 94.

[6] Quoted in Crawford, "John Mercer Langston," M. A. Thesis, Virginia State College (Petersburg, Va., 1940), 24, from George F. Bragg, *Hero of Jerusalem* (Baltimore, 1926), 5.

[7] Richmond *Virginia Star*, March 27, 1880.

rights of the bondholders in the name of Virginia's unspotted honor." [8]

It early became apparent to the Negro that his best interests lay with the Readjusters. At the party organizational meeting held by the Readjusters in Richmond on February 25, 1879, a few Negroes were present from Halifax and New Kent counties "in response to the call which convened the people of Virginia without distinction of color." [9] In spite of this bravely liberal beginning on the part of the Readjusters, like the Funders they ignored the Negroes until September, 1879, when Parson John E. Massey, implied in a speech at Petersburg that the Negroes would be welcomed into Readjuster ranks.[10] But because political identification with the Negroes had previously constituted political suicide, "the Readjusters sought the aid of the colored vote cautiously, well aware of the danger of raising the race issue." [11] It was not until late in the campaign that Negroes were openly invited to cooperate with the Readjusters and were promised more civil rights than the Funders would give them. In retaliation the Funders adopted similar tactics and ran Republican candidates in a number of counties in an effort to split the Negro vote.[12] At Lynchburg, John W. Daniel, later U. S. Senator, proved himself to be as politically adept as the Readjusters. While speaking to a Negro audience he seized the hands of two Negro preachers on the platform with him and advanced to the front of the stage, declaring, "When the best men of both races unite in a cause it must prevail." [13]

If such brotherly demonstrations seemed heretical to many Conservatives, they could always identify themselves with United States Senator Robert E. Withers, who wrote in his autobiography of the 1879 campaign:

> I thought the Petersburg meeting afforded a suitable occasion for raising the flag of the white race in the face of the large crowd of negroes present. I took, therefore, an early opportunity to declare that in my canvass, I did not propose to ask, nor did I expect to receive

---

[8] C. Vann Woodward, *Origins of the New South, 1877–1913*, vol. IX of *A History of the South*, edited by Wendell H. Stephenson and E. Merton Coulter (Louisiana State University, 1951), 67–68.
[9] Blake, *William Mahone*, 182.
[10] Morton, *Negro in Virginia Politics*, 107.
[11] Eckenrode, "History of Virginia Since 1865," p. 137.
[12] Blake, *William Mahone*, 182.
[13] Pendleton, *History of Appalachian Virginia*, 345.

the vote of any Negro, that however honest might be their purposes, they neither possessed information or [sic] intelligence to enable them to decide matters of state craft, and for this I did not hold them accountable. I said that Virginia had always been governed by white men, and I was determined to perpetuate their rule. This declaration was received with many growls of dissent from the blacks in the audience, but was vociferously cheered by the white men.[14]

With many Funders holding such anti-Negro views, and with nearly ten years of Conservative rule to remind Negroes of that party's attitude toward them, it was not surprising that the majority of Negroes who voted cast their ballots for the Readjuster ticket. Many Negroes in ignorance voted for the Readjusters because they thought the new party was going to readjust the Negro-white relationship.[15] But a far greater number of Negroes voted the Readjuster ticket because,

> The Readjusters said to the Negroes, 'Put us in office and we will keep your schools open, pay your teachers, provide for your higher education, abolish the whipping post, and remove your insane from jails to a well equipped asylum.' And they did it. These were the motives controlling the Negroes when they went to the polls in 1879.[16]

It is doubtful, however, whether the Negro vote was critical, much less the deciding factor in the Readjuster victory. "Possibly if no negro votes had been cast, the Readjusters would have won, though by a small majority. The negroes who voted with them voted for the schools." [17] Every senatorial district west of the Blue Ridge Mountains, with the exception of Augusta county, returned a Readjuster senator. In that whole region there were 68,500 white voters to only 9,000 colored voters. Certainly the Negro did not put the Readjusters in power there. That they represented a popular, democratic movement was indicated by the fact that wherever a large percentage of the qualified voters went to the polls, the Readjusters won. In

---

[14] Robert E. Withers, *Autobiography of an Octogenarian* (Roanoke, Virginia, 1907), 248–249.

[15] Writers Program of the Work Projects Administration, *The Negro in Virginia* (New York, 1940), 234.

[16] James Hugo Johnston, "The Participation of Negroes in the Government of Virginia from 1877 to 1888," *The Journal of Negro History*, IX, (July, 1929), 255.

[17] Eckenrode, "History of Virginia Since 1865," pp. 139–140.

Augusta, the most conservative of the upper Valley counties and the one most like the eastern counties in its social make-up, only thirty-three percent of the qualified electorate voted, and there the Funders won their lone victory in western Virginia. In neighboring Rockbridge, where sixty-four percent of the qualified electorate voted, the Readjusters won by a large majority. East of the Blue Ridge, in the northern Piedmont, the regular organization was more successful, and there only a small percentage bothered to vote, giving the Funders victory.[18]

Oddly enough, the total vote was small, only 143,000—82,000 for the Readjusters and 61,000 for the Funders.[19] Two years later, in the gubernatorial election when the issues were essentially the same, it rose to 211,000.[20]

After the election, the Readjusters became increasingly aware of the value, as well as danger, of having Negro allies. W. Z. T. Epperson, writing to S. Y. Gilliam concerning Readjuster party organization in Dinwiddie County, declared that "[We should] throw out every inducement to the leading colored people in the county." Epperson immediately emphasized that this was not intended to mean social equality, and then continued:

. . . without them, we can do nothing within ourselves, for we are weak as yet, and need all the assistance we can possibly get. . . . Now is the time for us, as readjusters . . . to coax the colored people into our party. . . .
And we need not care what means we may use either, since the funders have read all honest thinking readjusters out of their party.[21]

The Readjuster movement had indeed restored the Negro to political prominence. With the Conservatives split into Funders and Readjusters, the Negro at times found himself holding the balance of power in many local areas. The Readjusters appreciated this fact and actively sought Negro support. Some minor political offices, especially in the Black Belt, were turned over to them, but no special

[18] George M. McFarland, "Extension of Democracy in Virginia," Ph.D. Dissertation (Princeton University, 1934), 125.
[19] Eckenrode, "History of Virginia Since 1865," p. 138.
[20] Blake, *William Mahone*, 189.
[21] W. Z. T. Epperson to S. Y. Gilliam, December 23, 1879. Thomas Staples Martin Political Papers (Collection of James A. Bear, Jr., Charlottesville, Virginia).

effort was made to elevate the Negro and none was given important office by the Readjusters. Readjuster rule meant a greater measure of justice for the Negro, but nowhere did it mean Negro rule.[22]

Opposed to the Readjuster-controlled legislature was the staunchly Funder governor, F. W. M. Holliday. Readjuster legislation which got past Funder delaying tactics such as repeated rollcalls, motions for adjournment, and daily reading in full of the previous day's journal, was almost certain to be vetoed by Governor Holliday.[23] For two years, the Readjusters were stymied at every turn. Not till 1882, when the life of the Readjuster-controlled legislature was half over, was that party able to put into practice any significant part of its political principles. This partial success was made possible by the election, in the previous November of William E. Cameron of Petersburg, the Readjuster candidate for governor. He had beaten the Funder candidate, John W. Daniel, by a majority of 11,716 votes out of a total of 211,230.[24] The Readjusters had retained control in the Senate by twenty-three to seventeen, and in the House by fifty-eight to forty-two. Three of the Senators and eleven of the Delegates were Negroes.[25] Politically and racially, the legislature elected in 1881 was almost numerically identical to that elected in 1879. Largely as a result of Governor Holliday's veto, the first Readjuster legislature had been thwarted, but by the election of a Readjuster governor and another Readjuster legislature, the people demonstrated their continued sympathy and identification with Readjuster principles.

With the election of Cameron, a flood-tide of liberal measures broke upon Virginia such as she had not seen before and was not to see after. The poll tax was abolished as a voting prerequisite and its helpmate, the whipping post, was eliminated. Because anyone who had been legally whipped was barred from voting, that punishment had been increasingly inflicted upon Negro offenders. The state tax code was revised; the tax rate was lowered from fifty to forty cents per-thousand dollars of assessed value; delinquent taxes against the well-to-do were collected; railroads' taxable values had tripled and

[22] Martin, "Negro Disfranchisement in Virginia," *Howard University Studies in the Social Sciences*, I, pp. 92–93; Eckenrode, "History of Virginia Since 1865," 165; Charles C. Pearson, *The Readjuster Movement in Virginia*, 151.
[23] Munford, *Random Recollections*, 151–152.
[24] Blake, *William Mahone*, 189.
[25] Pendleton, *History of Appalachian Virginia*, 348.

they became liable for local taxes. A state institution of higher learning for Negroes was established, and a Negro asylum for the insane was opened. Public school appropriations were increased by half, closed schools were reopened, and back teacher salaries were paid. Labor unions were chartered, and regulations on the bonding of insurance companies tightened, while Granger proposals received a sympathetic hearing.[26]

The need for this legislation had long been ignored by the Funders. As conservative extremists they were willing to sacrifice social services, including the public schools and indeed anything else, in order to pay the debt and then hew to the basic principles of reaction and retrenchment.[27] To this group of old Democrats and Whiggish conservatives—known as the Funder wing of the Conservative party—such legislation was anathema, but it rescued the state from social and economic despair. When the dynamic Readjuster party was repudiated two years later, however, their rejection was due to more than malicious and false Funder charges of Negro domination; it was also due to consistently high-handed political practices by Mahone and his followers—including joining the Republicans. By the time of the election of 1883, the Readjuster party had largely fulfilled its promises and its destiny. Lacking a continued, liberal program, it fell apart from within while wrangling over division of the spoils and over future leadership.

One of the most popular pieces of Readjuster legislation—with white and black—was repeal of the constitutional amendment of 1876 which established poll tax payment as a prerequisite to voting. Plainly aimed at the Negro, a highly restricted suffrage also fitted the political ideals of conservative leaders who had kept property qualifications on the suffrage till 1851, making Virginia, along with North Carolina, one of the last two states to adopt the democratic principle of universal, white, manhood suffrage.

In 1874, 14 percent of the assessed whites and 41 percent of the assessed Negroes, had failed to pay the poll tax, whose proceeds were used for support of the public school system. In 1875, the year before poll tax payment was made a prerequisite to voting, 14.8 percent of the assessed whites and 37.3 percent of the assessed Negroes

---

[26] Blake, *William Mahone*, 192; Writers Program of the WPA, *Negro in Virginia*, 234; Woodward, *Origins of the New South*, 95–96.
[27] Woodward, *Origins of the New South*, 61.

failed to pay the poll tax. This was the state-wide percentage. In the cities the delinquency rate was much higher; 39.7 percent and 72.7 percent for assessed whites and Negroes, respectively, in 1875.[28] As was intended, the amendment reduced, but only slightly, the number of Negro voters. It also reduced the number of white voters—a prospect its framers could hardly have failed to foresee. Thus in 1881, the year before the amendment was repealed, the delinquency rate was 17.2 percent for the whites and 42.8 percent for the Negroes,[29] or an increase of 2.4 percent for the whites and 5.5 percent for the Negroes over the year 1875, just before the amendment was adopted. The Richmond *State* on November 18, 1882, claimed that

. . . the poll tax requirement kept at least one fourth of our white voters from the polls, simply because of their neglect to pay the tax or their refusal to allow anyone to pay it for them; while on the other hand the colored voter had somebody to attend to this small matter for him, and was not at all sensitive about it.[30]

Neither the white nor the colored vote was greatly reduced by the amendment. Perhaps the chief result of the amendment was the increase in election corruption. Political agents often paid the tax for both black and white, and Negroes who voted sensibly, *i.e.* for Conservatives, were often not required to pay.[31] The English visitor, Sir George Campbell, was told that collectors were often deliberately lax in their collection of poll taxes till after elections were over.[32] Poll taxes often were not assessed against Negroes, or when payment was offered by them, it might be refused.[33]

Opposition to the poll tax amendment came from the poor whites as well as from the Negroes. Especially was there strong white opposition in the Republican counties of the West.[34] The Readjuster legislative sessions of both 1879–1880 and 1880–1881, passed resolutions for repeal of the amendment. In November, 1882, the people endorsed these resolutions and repealed the poll tax amendment by

---

[28] Snavely, *Taxation of Negroes in Virginia*, 16.
[29] *Ibid.*, 21.
[30] Quoted in Snavely, *Taxation of Negroes in Virginia*, 20.
[31] Martin, "Negro Disfranchisement in Virginia," *Howard University Studies in the Social Sciences*, I, p. 86.
[32] Sir George Campbell, *White and Black: The Outcome of a Visit to the United States* (New York, 1879), 283.
[33] Richmond *Weekly Whig*, June 16, 1882.
[34] Martin, "Negro Disfranchisement in Virginia," *Howard University Studies in the Social Sciences*, I, p. 87.

a vote of 107,303 to 66,131. This vote was somewhat smaller than the one which had approved the amendment in 1876, by a vote of 129,373 to 98,359.[35]

From the Readjusters, the Virginia Negro for the first time received a measure of justice. In 1882, the well-known journalist, J. B. Harrison, did a series of articles for the *Atlantic Monthly* entitled "Studies in the South." While noting that Negroes in Mississippi, Louisiana, and southern Alabama were not allowed to vote without a great deal of obstruction, he wrote that he found no such conditions of oppression or obstruction in Virginia. A conservative himself, who idealized the life of the Southern rural gentleman as "the most pleasing imaginable," Harrison generally condemned the Readjusters,[36] refusing to attribute to them credit for the better conditions of the Negro which he noted in Virginia. Virginia Negroes knew, however, who their real friends were. The following excerpt is from an address to the Negro voters of Virginia, urging them to vote the Readjuster ticket in 1883, which was signed by more than three-hundred Negroes:

> . . . the Democratic party has . . . lost no opportunity to oppress us; to disfranchise us by means of the whipping-post, the payment of capitation taxes and other class legislation. . . . They . . . [made] petit larceny an offense, for the commission of which even the smallest boy would be disfranchised forever. The whipping-post was an easy road to the disfranchisement of the black men. . . . This hateful system went on, until today we have about eight thousand blacks disfranchised.
>
> What has the Readjuster Party done? They found the whipping-post a relic of the barbarous ages . . . [and] wiped it away. . . . They found that a man was compelled to pay $1 before he could vote, and in many instances he could not find the Democratic tax collector when he wanted to pay this tax to vote, if the collector knew he was not going to vote his way. . . . [The Readjusters] wiped away that requirement which . . . by Democratic manipulations, had disfranchised thousands of colored voters. . . .
>
> They found that our lunatics were kept in barracks . . . a relic of the war, and now little better than horse stables . . . they gave us $100,000 to build an asylum for . . . our insane, and $56,000 an-

---

[35] Snavely, *Taxation of Negroes in Virginia*, 18, 20.
[36] J. B. Harrison, "Studies in the South," *Atlantic Monthly*, L (1882), 102–103.

nually for the support of this institution . . . they appropriated $100,000 for the building of a college for the education of our sons and daughters, and put the management and control of this institution entirely in the hands of colored men, and today that institution is open. . . .

They gave us fifteen colored men as guards at the state penitentiary. They gave us a colored man as assistant post-master at Norfolk. . . . colored men as members of school trustee boards [and] colored men as jurors.[37]

Said the Negro newspaper, the Washington, D. C., *Bee*, of Mahone and the Readjusters:

Mahone has . . . made it safe for a man to be a Republican in Virginia if he wants to, and he has been mainly instrumental in compelling better schools for the children, and a show of justice for all men regardless of color or politics.[38]

Virginia Negroes knew that the following political charge made by H. H. Riddleberger was true and not just partisan politics:

By a system of trickery, through disqualifications for petty offenses, and requiring the payment of a head tax as a prerequisite to voting, and using every means to prevent its payment, they [the Conservatives] had virtually disfranchised the negro, and by a system of frauds in the counting and certifying of returns they had guarded against any accidents resulting from his casting a vote. The system was too complete to require any violence.[39]

And following the defeat of the Readjusters in 1883, the Negro *Lancet* of Petersburg lamented:

The Readjusters are the only men who have been of any substantial benefit to . . . [the Negroes.] The Republicans could not, and the Bourbons would not, befriend them.[40]

Justice, not Negro rule, had gained for the Readjusters this high

---

[37] "An address to the colored voters of the State of Virginia," signed by State Senators W. N. Stevens, D. N. Norton, and J. R. Jones; eleven members of the House of Delegates; seven ex-members of the legislature; and two-hundred eighty-six persons from throughout the state; *A Documentary History of the Negro People in the United States*, edited by Herbert Aptheker (New York, 1951), 732–734.

[38] Washington, D. C. *Bee*, January 20, 1883.

[39] H. H. Riddleberger, "Bourbonism in Virginia," *North American Review*, CXXXIV (1882), 425.

[40] Petersburg *Lancet*, November 24, 1883.

regard in Negro circles. In 1881, the Readjuster organ, the Richmond *Whig*, pointed out that in more than a third of the Virginia
counties Negroes were in a majority, and in some of them overwhelmingly so, hence placing those counties "at the mercy of a
colored and Republican voting majority." But, said the *Whig*, the
Negroes and Republicans were placing white men, not black, in
county offices—and often white Conservatives.[41] No Negro was ever
appointed to a key administrative post and the few Negro appointments made by the Readjusters were invariably to minor, unimpor-
tant positions.[42]

Gross distortion of historical fact by newspapers and contempo-
raries is the basis of the popular image of Negro rule during the
Readjuster years, 1879–1883. Such statements as the following,
though made privately, have distorted the overall picture of the
Readjuster years. General W. H. Payne of Warrenton, wrote to
John W. Daniel in 1881:

> I am inclined to the opinion that men like us must retire from the
> higher walks of politics. We must give place to our Readjuster *friends*
> who are willing to subordinate the debt to the 'nigger question.' [43]

From Senator W. C. Butler of South Carolina, a former Confederate
major-general, came the advice and "call to the colors,"

> [To defeat Mahone and the Readjusters] What you need to do is to
> organize your *young* men under an agressive prudent leader, who will
> bring out a full white vote.
>
> Your next fight is the fight of the whole South and we shall watch
> it with much anxiety and interest.[44]

In but a few local areas was anything resembling Negro rule
even approached. In 1875, four years before the Readjusters came
to power, Edward King noted such an instance in Petersburg, as
well as the reactions of the whites to it.

> At Petersburg the negroes are from time to time largely represented
> in the Common Council, and sometimes have a controlling voice in
> municipal affairs. The white citizens have readily adapted themselves

---

[41] Richmond *Weekly Whig*, April 1, 1881.
[42] Eckenrode, "History of Virginia Since 1865," p. 165; Pearson, *Readjuster
Movement in Virginia*, 151.
[43] W. H. Payne to John W. Daniel, April 9, 1881. John W. Daniel Papers
(Duke University Library).
[44] W. C. Butler to John W. Daniel, May 16, 1881. Daniel Papers.

to circumstances and the session of the Council which I attended was as orderly and, in the main, as well conducted as that of any Eastern city. Most of the colored members were full types of the African. The Commissioner of Streets and Engineer of the Board of Waterworks were both negroes. The mayoralty and the other city offices remained . . . in the hands of the white Radicals.[45]

In the Readjuster legislature the role and votes of the Negro members were at times vital. For instance, the act of April 21, 1882, which abolished the whipping post, might not have become law but for the efforts of Senator J. Richard Jones of Mecklenburg county.[46] And contrary to popular opinion, the Negro members of the legislature proved by their efforts that they represented all the people of their constituencies and not just the Negroes. The brothers Robert and Daniel Norton, the former in the House and the latter in the Senate, and together or singly representing York, James City, Elizabeth City, and Warwick counties, collaborated in introducing a bill to define the boundary between Warwick and Elizabeth City and also on another bill giving Virginia's consent to the national government to purchase the Cornwallis surrender site at Yorktown for a national monument.[47] Other non-race legislation introduced by Negro members, both before and during the Readjuster era, included a fence law, conservation of fish and oysters in Chesapeake Bay, prohibition of drinking by minors, anti-gambling legislation, free bridges, repair of the State Capitol, maintenance of houses of correction, limited hunting seasons on partridges and deer, etc.[48] This is not meant to deny, however, that the chief concerns of the Negro legislators were the welfare of their race, primarily with regard to (1) travel on common carriers, (2) landlord-tenant relationships, (3) jury service, (4) treatment of prisoners, (5) the whipping post, (6) civil rights, and (7) lynching.[49]

Mahone and the Readjusters actively sought Negro support in the legislative campaign of 1883. If there was ever any doubt that history would cover the name of Mahone in obloquy, this campaign removed it. One scholar has written that by this time, "In the eyes of

---

[45] King, *The Great South*, 580–581.
[46] Luther P. Jackson, *Negro Office-Holders in Virginia, 1865–1895* (Norfolk, Virginia, 1945), 81.
[47] *Ibid.*, 79.
[48] *Ibid.*, 75–80.
[49] *Ibid.*, 74.

many Virginians of all classes, Mahone was a sort of renegade—worst of all, a leader of negroes." [50]

It was also in this election that Conservatives abandoned both the names "Conservative" and "Funder," and for the first time since the war called themselves Democrats—which must have been painful to some of the old-line Whigs now in their ranks. As a result of the reforms instituted by the Readjusters and the justice which they had accorded the Negro, the Democrats knew it would be hopeless to try to divide the Negro vote. So instead, they drew the color line and made race the dominant note of the campaign. Declared John W. Daniel: "I am a Democrat because I am a white man and a Virginian." [51] The issue in the campaign appeared to be solely that of race. For the Democrats no more successful one could have been devised. Even with the dissension, the sometimes demonstrated incompetence and dishonesty, and the lack of a continued and expanded program of reform within Readjuster ranks, it is doubtful that any other issue could have turned the Readjusters out of office.

Such a campaign provided the perfect setting for the Danville Riot of November 4, 1883, just a few days before the election took place. Indeed the riot may even have been the peroration of the Democratic campaign, the direct result of the so-called Democratic Circular, allegedly written by a group of white businessmen in Danville, which complained of Negro domination, humiliation, and unjust treatment of the white people of Danville. Following the riot, Cornelius H. Fauntleroy, student at the University of Virginia and descendant of the old German pioneer, Jost Hite, wrote home to his grandmother near Winchester in the Valley:

The Danville Circular and Riot won the day in Virginia. The former was the greatest fraud ever published to a confiding public. Some unessential particulars were true, but the main statements were either out and out lies, or the grossest exaggerations. There is almost indubitable grounds for the belief that the circular was concocted many days or months *before* the time it was issued in Danville, with a view to springing it on the people just before the election and too late for its falsehood to be exposed. If it had been promulgated ten days *sooner*, it would have been *riddled* on every stump by the Readjuster speakers,

[50] Eckenrode, "History of Virginia Since 1865," p. 172.
[51] Morton, *Negro in Virginia Politics*, 119; Martin, "Negro Disfranchisement in Virginia," *Howard University Studies in the Social Sciences*, I, p. 97.

and by the Readjuster press. It would have fallen *flat*. This they knew full well. Hence the trick.[52]

How or where Fauntleroy got his information is not clear. Nor is it known exactly who or what was to blame for starting the Danville Riot. No two accounts today read alike, and certainly no two news-papers of the day reported it alike, except that almost all the Virginia papers, other than the *Whig*, laid all the blame on the Negroes and the Readjusters. The U. S. Senate felt that the riot had been serious enough to warrant an investigation, in which the city of Danville was ably defended by Senator Zebulon B. Vance of North Carolina. The conditions under which the riot occurred were complicated. A South-side city in the heart of the Black Belt, Danville had a population of about 8,000, slightly more than half of them Negroes. Until 1882, the city had remained under the definite control of the white popula-tion, but during the Readjuster regime of Mahone the city was divided into wards. As a result the Negroes gained a majority in the twelve-man council, and four of the nine policemen were colored, as were all or nearly all of the justices-of-the-peace. The super-intendent of the public market was a Negro, and Negroes domi-nated that place, having rented twenty of the twenty-four stalls. On the other hand, however, the mayor, judge, commonwealth's attorney, city sergeant, constable, commissioner of revenue, and chief of police, as well as other officials, were all white. Nevertheless, it was noised about that Danville had a Negro government, and then the Danville Circular appeared. The white mayor, when interviewed by a *Whig* reporter, refuted most of these charges, although it is quite possible that the Democratic organization was responsible for the circular in an attempt to intimidate the Negro and solidify white sentiment against him. Finally excitement began to grow in the whole state over conditions in Danville. For the first time it was charged that the local government of a sizable and populous area was under Negro rule. The presence of Negro officials in many parts of the state was not new, but the belief that Danville had fallen under Negro rule was, and the city became a powder keg.

Negroes were normally expected to step aside when they en-

---

[52] Cornelius H. Fauntleroy to (Mrs.) Elizabeth A. Hite, November 27, 1883. Cornelius Baldwin Hite, Jr., Papers (Duke University Library). See also Martin, "Negro Disfranchisement in Virginia," *Howard University Studies in the Social Sciences*, I, p. 97 for support of this contention.

countered white people on the city's sidewalks. They had adopted the practice, however, of deliberately jostling white people instead whenever there were strong feelings on controversial issues, as was always the case during political campaigns. And sometimes white women were allegedly pushed into the gutters of unpaved streets. On November 4, a Negro jostled a white man on the streets of Danville. An argument followed, and in the ensuing fight the white man drew a revolver and fired. More firing by others followed—certainly by white men, since nearly everyone carried pistols then; whether or not any of the Negroes fired pistols is not certain, but it was the custom for many of them to carry straight razors. When the fighting was all over, one white man lay dying and four others were wounded. Four Negroes were dead and six had been wounded. Governor Cameron called out the militia, but before it arrived, order returned and what Virginians called Mahoneism had been dealt a fatal blow.[53]

Further evidence of Democratic chicanery in the Danville affair came in the form of a wire sent to all parts of the Southwest—a Readjuster and Republican stronghold—on the day following the riot. It read:

> We are standing in our doors [in Danville] with shot guns in hand, defending our wives and children from an organized mob of negroes now parading the streets!

But the Richmond *Whig* declared that "a colored man was not to be seen in the streets of Danville on that day." [54]

Masterfully conceived and executed, the Democratic strategy was a complete success. Thoroughly intimidated, large numbers of Negroes stayed away from the polls in a quiet election with an otherwise heavy turn-out. The Democrats won a two-thirds majority in both houses of the legislature,[55] partly due to the perpetration of election frauds on an even grander scale than usual.

Mahone, bitter, angry, and frustrated at the dissension in his own ranks no less than he was at the Democrats, lashed out at the latter for the tactics they had resorted to:

---

[53] Eckenrode, "History of Virginia Since 1865," pp. 182–184; Morton, *Negro in Virginia Politics*, 119–121; Martin, "Negro Disfranchisement in Virginia," *Howard University Studies in the Social Sciences*, I, p. 97; Pearson, *Readjuster Movement in Virginia*, 164. (The most impartial account is Eckenrode.)

[54] Quoted in Martin, "Negro Disfranchisement in Virginia," *Howard University Studies in the Social Sciences*, I, p. 98.

[55] Morton, *Negro in Virginia Politics*, 121.

When the Bourbon faction assembled in Lynchburg in July last to formulate a platform, a large element of its membership avowedly and openly favored the adoption of the "color line." Bourbon journals claimed that the true issue of the canvass was the race issue, and that the contest should be forced into a struggle between the whites and blacks . . . for reasons best known to themselves, the Bourbons . . . determined not to make written proclamation of their purpose to draw the color line. . . . The temporary chairman of the convention addressed himself to "the white people of Virginia"; leading Bourbon organs recommended the platform adopted as a "white man's platform". . . the whole burden of the Bourbon leaders in the white districts was to excite the race prejudices and passions of the whites against the blacks.[56]

Shortly following the election, Mahone received a letter from a U. S. Department of Justice official who signed the communication with only the letters "B. N. B." Deploring the condition of the Virginia Negro, this person wrote,

. . . the purpose [of the Danville Riot] was to spread dismay among the poor blacks, and drive them from the polls, and to terrorize the whites, and relax their faith in you and your mission.

. . . the negro's condition is worse now than it was before [the war. Then] the white man owned him, and he treated him with some consideration, and was his friend. But now the white man is his enemy.[57]

From November 1883 on, there was no doubt—if indeed there had ever been—about the place of the Virginia Negro. Speaking to a public gathering in Lynchburg following the Danville Riot, former Confederate General Jubal A. Early, declared that, "The negroes must know that they are to behave themselves and keep in their proper places."[58] "Falkland," in *vox populi* of the Whig, deplored the fact that ". . . Bourbonism has succeeded once again in raising aloft in triumph the black flag of intolerance. . . ."[59]

Letters to Mahone began to reveal the extent of fraud and intimidation practiced by the Democrats in the late election. From Halifax Court House came one mournful lament:

[56] Richmond *Weekly Whig*, November 23, 1883.
[57] B. N. B. to William Mahone, November 11, 1883. William A. Mahone Papers (Duke University Library).
[58] Pearson, *Readjuster Movement in Virginia*, 164.
[59] Richmond *Weekly Whig*, November 23, 1883.

It is a painful thing to me to write you how infamous the funders have acted in this county. They have carried the election here by fraud, intimidation, shooting, and cutting the negroes. The funders went to the election . . . swearing they would kill the negroes. The negroes have no protection here. They are scared now and I think most of them would leave the country if they could.[60]

A week later, the same correspondent again wrote to Mahone,

. . . the principle [sic] argument of [the] funders was mixed schools, mixed marriages, mixed society, and a war of races. I know of a number of negroes that will loose [sic] their homes on account of their politics. The funders in a number of places rode around day before the election and told the negroes if they went to the election they would be shot. We have lost at least 160 negro votes by the committee striking off names from the Registration books . . . and at least 60 votes by the funders paying them from $2 to $5 to stay at home and not vote . . . the funders had their whiskey by the five gallons and made a number of negroes drunk and led them to the polls like sheep to the slaughter . . . we have no one to prosecute the offenders.[61]

From Front Royal, central gateway to the Valley, came word that,

. . . it is almost impossible to prove the facts because these colored people know if they inform against the Bourbons they . . . will make it *intolerable for them here in the future.* [Also] . . . some [whites] were frightened by the "race issue" into voting the Funder ticket.[62]

In a sworn statement, Lewis Oliver, Petersburg Negro, testified that J. P. Williamson, Petersburg candidate for the House of Delegates on the Democratic ticket, said to him when meeting him on the street following the election: "Where have you been? You have been dodging me." When Oliver replied, "No Sir," Williamson continued,

. . . you did not want to vote for me, that is about the truth of it! It was your duty to vote for me—you have been getting your bread from me!

Just look at your friends in Danville, see how they were shot down

---

[60] J. D. Clay to William Mahone, November 12, 1883. Mahone Papers.
[61] *Ibid.*, November 19, 1883.
[62] C. L. Pritchard to William Mahone, November 19, 1883. Mahone Papers.

there the other day—This is a white man's country, and they are going to rule it.[63]

The years that followed 1883 were years of reaction for the Virginia Negro, for that year represented the high tide of liberalism
in Virginia. Mahone was to remain on the scene in Virginia politics
till the day of his death, October 8, 1895, although long before that
date he had become a mere myth, a bogey, a fear to be conjured with
at every election, but a threat no less. Long before then, the Negroes
had turned against him, and he supposedly against them. But in
1883, the Negro owed a tremendous debt to the dapper, dictatorial,
little political manipulator, who possessed genuine qualities of realistic statemanship. Repeatedly he crossed the political stage during
the years 1883–1895, but more often he appeared only in the wings.

Mahone's character and role in a much misunderstood era, have
been unfairly maligned. Mahone was dynamic, able, and controversial. That he succeeded in a liberal, political program for even a brief
period in the Virginia of that day, is a testament to those qualities.
Except for his outstanding war record, which was often enviously
denied him, he possessed none of the prerequisites for Virginia
leadership of that day. His family name had been unknown to the
mass of Virginians for he was the son of a tavernkeeper. And tavern-
keeping was not a gentleman's profession in the South. Physically
Mahone could hardly have commanded respect. Virginia leaders
usually *looked* the role, whereas he stood about five-feet-five inches
tall and weighed less than a hundred pounds. Early identifying himself with personal and ambitious designs upon railroad consolidation
in Virginia, he hardly could have endeared himself to Virginia
lawyer-gentry forced by hard times to serve as retainers for
Northern interests. Mahone knew this and surrounded himself with
other, and usually lesser, self-made men, who had like himself risen
from nothing in the years from 1860 on.

Perhaps foremost among Mahone's real shortcomings was a domi-
neering, dictatorial manner. He acted as if he were running a railroad
or commanding an army, when he was in reality trying to hold to-

---

[63] Sworn statement of Lewis Oliver before F. Gallagher, U. S. Commissioner for
the Eastern District of Virginia, November 24, 1883. Mahone Papers. In the
Mahone Papers, November 21–30, 1883, in folder labeled "Election Frauds," are
dozens of sworn statements of fraud and intimidation of Negroes in the November,
1883 election.

gether one of the most heterogeneous political followings any Virginian ever had—realistic white Conservatives, white and black Republicans who had despaired of their own party's success, wage-earners, and small farmers from every part of Virginia. Mahone was a political manipulator who worked best from behind the scenes. The democratic give-and-take necessary for holding such a disparate group together was foreign to his nature and training. Starting at the top, Mahone alienated his chief lieutenants, such as Parson Massey, apparently because Mahone regarded Massey as a threat to his pre-eminence.[64] And if by his general peremptoriness he had not already alienated a large part of his rank-and-file, he sealed the doom of the conglomerate coalition that was the Readjuster party by casting his lot with the Republicans in the U. S. Senate in 1881. Notwithstanding the fact that the Conservatives (Funders) had read him out of the party, it was the height of political folly if Mahone believed he could, as a Republican, continue to command a Conservative following. Especially was this true since the problem which had brought him that following, the state debt, apparently had been settled by the Riddleberger Act of 1882.

All of these factors contributed to the picture of apostate and renegade, dictator and "Negro lover," generally presented in the writings of his contemporaries. The absence of a friendly press helped to draw such a picture, for, with few exceptions, notably the Richmond *Whig*, the Abingdon *Virginian*, and the Luray *Page Courier*, the press of the state was overwhelmingly conservative and anti-Mahone.

J. L. M. Curry, a leading Funder, felt that the Mahone regime had inflicted irreparable disgrace upon the good name of Virginia. It would have been defeated sooner, however, thought Curry, had Mahone not received aid from "ill-informed" Northerners. Claiming that the 1883 defeat of Mahone and the Readjusters would have been even more crushing but for support given Mahone by President Arthur, Curry said he had never seen such rejoicing as took place—apparently in Richmond—following the election. "Old men wept. The young were hilarious. The women thanked God." [65] On the

---

[64] See Withers, *Autobiography*, 382, and Elizabeth H. Hancock, editor, *Autobiography of John E. Massey*, 193–194.
[65] J. L. M. Curry to R. C. Winthrop, November 8, 1883. J. L. M. Curry Papers (Library of Congress, Washington, D. C.).

other hand, Lewis H. Blair, Richmond businessman and undoubtedly the most liberal-minded critic of his state in that day, summarized the achievements and results of Mahoneism in quite a different light. Reminding his readers that when Mahone came to power there were employed by the state in Richmond five members of one family, Blair continued:

> General Mahone . . . marshalled all the forces in opposition, and soon had almost as undisputed sway as his predecessors previously had. The rotten dead wood was swept aside, and although the new party had many sins, arising principally because its power was also absolute . . . it cannot be fairly claimed that the new order of affairs was worse than the old. We then had so-called negro rule, but the Commonwealth survived, and in the opinion of many, was much benefited.[66]

In the twentieth century, a Negro historian ably summed up the enigma of Mahone. James Hugo Johnston wrote in 1929:

> Inasmuch as the Virginians followed this leader by a large majority in 1879 an inquiry into their political sanity would make an interesting study. It must seem strange to find an ex-Confederate general, courting the vote of the Negro, while other ex-Confederate leaders condemned such action and denounced the activity of Negro politicians. The student would like to know whether this man was the infamous demagogue plotting for self alone, or whether he, living in that day of rabid race hate, was an enlightened and far sighted student of public affairs, who unlike his fellows, saw farther than they and determined that white and Negro Virginians should work in political union for mutual good and for a better Virginia.[67]

W. H. T. Squires, a normally conservative Virginia historian, confessed that from a position of "intense prejudice" against Mahone, he concluded after study of him, "that he is . . . the most outrageously maligned character in V[irgini]a history."[68] Later, he said in a sketch of Mahone appearing in his *Land of Decision*, that

. . . no one ever loved Virginia more devotedly than he; none ever

---

[66] Lewis H. Blair, *The Prosperity of the South Dependent Upon the Elevation of the Negro* (Richmond, Virginia, 1889), 69.

[67] Johnston, "Participation of Negroes in the Government of Virginia. . . . 1877 to 1888," *Journal of Negro History*, XIV, p. 257.

[68] Quoted in Blake, *William Mahone*, p. 258 from a letter to L. L. Maury from Squires, July 2, 1930. Lucius L. Maury Papers (Courtland, Virginia.)

struggled so long and so successfully in so many different fields of achievement for Virginia, and no Virginian has received less gratitude and less appreciation.[69]

The noted Virginia historian, Hamilton J. Eckenrode, was remarkably sympathetic to Mahone in an unpublished, manuscript history of Virginia, written shortly before his death.[70]

Appearing arrogant and dictatorial to practically all of his critics,[71] Mahone possessed no great personal magnetism to endear him even to his friends.[72] A dyspeptic, senior, Confederate officer, he could, and did, keep a cow and chickens with him to offset the barely digestible fare of even the ranking officers' messes. Mahone was inclined to be quiet and uncommunicative.[73] Instead of angrily replying to malicious charges leveled at both him and the Readjuster party, he repeatedly said that he was content to leave his vindication to time, confident that sooner or later it would come.[74]

It was as a result, at least in part, of backstage manipulations by Mahone that Virginia was saved from Radical Reconstruction in 1869. It was due to his guiding, if at times heavy, hand that the Virginia Negro for a brief period in these turbulent years knew justice and was given something approaching an equal chance to qualify himself for the duties of manhood and democratic citizenship. (Mahone was too much of a realist, at that time at least, to push the Negro into higher office in return for votes.) It was due primarily to Mahone and his following that a readjustment and settlement of the state debt was achieved. And after the Funder element of the Conservatives returned to power, they were not willing to upset it for all of their past talk of "Virginia's unspotted honor." It was due to Mahone that Virginia knew liberal, progressive reforms in state legislation a decade before many of those same reforms were brought about in other Southern states as a result of either Populists in power or Populist agitation.

Slight indeed so far have been the vindication and recognition of

---

[69] W. H. T. Squires, *Land of Decision* (Portsmouth, Virginia, 1931), 200–201.

[70] Eckenrode, "History of Virginia Since 1865."

[71] Munford, *Random Recollections*, 148–149.

[72] John Herbert Claiborne, *Seventy-Five Years in Old Virginia* (New York, 1904), 239.

[73] *Ibid.*, 248.

[74] Blake, *William Mahone*, 256.

William Mahone, a man ahead of his time. His was the misfortune of being a political liberal and realist in an age of increasing conservatism which sought to escape reality by glorifying a halcyon past and creating the Confederate Cult.[75]

But in 1883, Virginia had by no means seen the last of Mahone, although his heyday was past. Neither had the Negro question been settled, nor had colored members been entirely removed from the state legislature. For years to come the race issue would mask other issues on which the people could have, and should have, divided. The Negro was down but not out. Still there should have been no doubt about the eventual outcome, for the Virginia Negro's heyday in the nineteenth century, like Mahone's, passed in November, 1883.

---

[75] In addition to the authorities and sources cited here as evidence to support this evaluation of Mahone, the general tenor of the Mahone Papers tends to support the evidence already presented.

Chapter 3

Reaction and the Triumph of One-Party Rule, 1884–1893

RESTORED to power by the state election of 1883, the Democratic party in Virginia resolutely set out to make itself safe from all threats to its supremacy. The Confederate tradition began to assume the proportions of a cult, and the pressure of the race issue rapidly increased.[1] As far as the Negro was concerned, the stage was set for reactionary measures which paved the way for his final disfranchisement in 1902.

Remembering Danville and the "Negro rule" which in fact that city never had, the Democratic legislature promptly amended the charters of cities like Danville and Petersburg so that Negro rule in the future would be an impossibility. Congressional districts were reapportioned so as to assure control by the Democratic party.[2] Readjuster Governor Cameron, in office till 1886, proved to be only a minor stumbling block. Democratic measures were simply repassed over his veto by the two-thirds majority in both houses. It was charged that this majority was arrived at by dubious, if not outright illegal, means *after* the legislature met,[3] *i.e.* by contested elections and Readjuster "resignations."

The highwater mark of proscriptive legislation was reached in the passage of a new election law sponsored by Delegate William A. Anderson, of Rockbridge county, and Senator J. Marshall McCormick, of Warren county. In both of these Valley counties the Negro was never present in large numbers. The original Anderson-McCormick law called for the election in 1884 and every four years thereafter, of three "freeholders" for each city and county who would in turn appoint local election officials. Nothing was said about party membership of either the "freeholders" or the local officials, but a Democratic legislature wrote the law. Governor Cameron vetoed the

---

[1] Eckenrode, "History of Virginia Since 1865," p. 205.
[2] Morton, *Negro in Virginia Politics*, 123.
[3] Pendleton, *History of Appalachian Virginia*, 358; Blake, *William Mahone*, 228.

bill, only to have it passed over his veto. Almost immediately, however, the new law was voided by the Court of Appeals for violating the state constitution by establishing a freehold or land-owning qualification. Not to be balked, the legislature forced the governor to call a special legislative session. It sat from August to early December, 1884, and from it emerged a new Anderson-McCormick law substantially the same as the original one, except that it was purged of the unconstitutional freehold qualification. By it Democratic party control of the state was assured and control of most local areas as well. The new law was an open invitation to fraud and corruption, and its passage marked the beginning of the wholesale ballot-box-stuffing which led the state, in shame and embarrassment, to pass another election law in 1894.[4] Of the 1884 law, the Richmond *Dispatch* frankly stated: "The Anderson-McCormick bill was passed in the interest of the white people of Virginia. . . . It is a white man's law. It operates to perpetuate the rule of the white man in Virginia." [5]

Meanwhile Mahone's Readjuster following had either rapidly returned to the Democratic party or followed him into the Republican party. The result was that his position was vastly weakened. Even the able John E. Massey, remembering slights by Mahone, returned to the Democrats and was nominated by them for lieutenant-governor in 1885, on the ticket with General Fitzhugh Lee, nephew of "Marse Robert." Massey proved himself as able a campaigner for the Democrats as he had been for the Readjusters. Speaking before a Danville audience in 1884, prior to the general election of that year, Massey said:

> Other parts of the state are looking to you with the warmest sympathy. You have set them an example worthy of imitation and they expect you to repeat it in the future.[6]

This recalled, of course, to memory the riot and the methods used the previous year to assure Democratic victory. Massey may even have intended for his remarks to have just that effect.

Race-baiters took their campaigns into the valleys and mountains of western Virginia and stirred up anti-Negro feelings in many

---

[4] Martin, "Negro Disfranchisement in Virginia," *Howard University Studies in the Social Sciences*, I, pp. 99–100; *Appleton's Annual Cyclopedia* (1884), 797.
[5] Quoted in Martin, "Negro Disfranchisement in Virginia," *Howard University Studies in the Social Sciences*, I, p. 100.
[6] Quoted in Eckenrode, "History of Virginia Since 1865," p. 198.

whites who rarely saw a Negro. On October 7, 1884, William M. Cabell of Buckingham spoke at the courthouse in Covington, beseeching the mountain whites to come up and help "his poor, negroridden county." [7]

On election day that year, in Richmond, where numerous Negroes bore such names as George Washington, Thomas Jefferson, and Andrew Jackson, election officials often challenged their identity and either outright kept them from voting or delayed them till the polls were closed.[8] With election affairs now almost completely in the hands of the Democrats, it was no wonder that Readjuster Governor Cameron could write of the election of 1884:

> No official reports reached me from any source of violence or ill-doing during the late election. Had such been the case I should have communicated the facts to the Legislature as in duty bound. That there were irregularities and frauds, here and there, I have heard and make no doubt. I never knew any election without them; but that they were not general the large vote cast is sufficient proof. The election was singularly free from disturbances.[9]

Governor Cameron should have known better than to contend that a large vote (totaling 285,000) was any indication of the election's honesty. The vote was large, yes, but in general elections, when the Presidency was at stake, the vote was always larger than in off-year elections.

In 1885, the first year the Anderson-McCormick election law was in effect, the Democrats swept the state. They elected Fitzhugh Lee governor over the Republican candidate, John S. Wise, and won an overwhelming majority in both houses of the legislature. In the Senate, they gained twenty-nine seats to eleven for the Republicans, the latter including one Independent white Republican and one Negro Republican. In the House, they won seventy-two seats to twenty-eight for the Republicans, only one of whom was a Negro.[10] Lee and Wise were both popular personalities. Wise received a majority in ninety-three counties, and his friends claimed that he was only defeated by fraud in the remaining seven counties, all located

---

[7] Richmond *Weekly Whig*, October 17, 1884.
[8] Eckenrode, "History of Virginia Since 1865," p. 189.
[9] Governor William E. Cameron to Captain James B. Gregory, January 3, 1885. Gregory Family Papers (University of Virginia Library).
[10] Blake, *William Mahone*, 232.

in the Black Belt.[11] But in the election of legislators, race was the issue. "The Republicans, try as they would, could never get away from it. If the Democrats did not press it, the negroes would bring it forward."[12] The usual charges of fraud were made, and with election machinery so rigidly in the hands of one party, undoubtedly many of the charges were true. The Richmond *Whig* claimed that in Norfolk alone, a thousand Negroes were deprived of their vote.[13]

After this election (1885) the Republican party steadily lost strength in the eastern part of the state, while the Democrats gained in strength and numbers, even among the Negroes. In some areas a white man who voted Republican came to be looked upon as a traitor to his race.[14] Even as early as January, 1885, before the Republican defeat, the Richmond *State* reported that the Democratic party was strong and growing among the Negroes of Charlotte county.[15] In despair and out of "accommodation," they increasingly voted with their old masters.

In reality, the Negro had ceased to be a threat to Democratic party rule. But because it was good politics, the *Dispatch*, during the presidential campaign of 1888, called on every white man to vote the Democratic ticket because he was white—the implication being that the Negroes were all voting for the Republican ticket because they were Negroes. Although the Democrats won nine (a figure later reduced to seven) of Virginia's eleven congressional seats that year, there is considerable evidence that Virginia would have gone Republican with the winning candidate, Benjamin Harrison, but for dissension in Republican party ranks of the state. The total state vote for Cleveland was 151,979, and for Harrison 150,449—a Democratic majority of only 1,530. Fraud undoubtedly figured in this election, as it always did, but apathy and dissension caused many Republicans not to bother to vote.[16]

It was also in this election that the first—and last—Negro was elected to the U. S. Congress from Virginia. The Fourth Congressional District was heavily Negro in population, and repeatedly its colored leaders had unsuccessfully sought the nomination for a

[11] *Ibid.*, 232, note 190.
[12] Eckenrode, "History of Virginia Since 1865," p. 208.
[13] Cited in *Ibid.*, 203.
[14] *Ibid.*, 227.
[15] Richmond *State*, January 29, 1885.
[16] Eckenrode, "History of Virginia Since 1865," pp. 224–225.

Negro candidate. In 1884, they had run an independent candidate who was badly defeated. Mahone was no more willing to sanction the nomination of a Negro for an important political office than were the Democrats. But in 1888, John Mercer Langston, the illegitimate son of Ralph Quarles (white) of Louisa county, and Lucy Langston, a favorite, freed slave of mixed Indian and Negro ancestry, sought the Republican nomination. Northern-reared and educated at Oberlin College, Langston was intelligent and capable. A lawyer by profession, he had recruited Negro troops during the Civil War and later served with the Freedmen's Bureau. He had been professor of law and dean of the law school at Howard University, United States minister to Haiti, and president of Virginia's only state Negro college, located at Petersburg. Arrogant and proud, he was determined that a largely Negro congressional district should be represented by a Negro. Opposed by Mahone, he ran as an Independent Republican against the regular Republican nominee and a Democrat, Edward C. Venable. Venable was counted in, but Langston successfully contested the election, although he was not seated till September 23, 1890, the last week of the long session of the Fifty-first Congress. Failing in his attempt at reelection that November, he sat as a lame-duck Representative till March 3, 1891, when his term ended. His congressional record was commendable and he has been called the one scholar among the twenty-two Negroes who served in Congress in the nineteenth century.[17]

The backers of both the regular Republican nominee and the Democratic candidate knew that Langston was a formidable opponent. Not surprisingly, the campaign was an unusually bitter one. Langston was guilty of particularly intemperate and unwise statements, such as advocacy of sexual intermingling of the races to produce a superior civilization. But rapid deterioration of relations between the races and an alleged marked increase in rape and other violence cannot safely be said to date from the campaigns of 1888 and 1889, nor especially from the candidacy of Langston.[18]

The year 1888 was a momentous one in Virginia politics because it was also in that year that the people first voted on the question of

---

[17] *Ibid.*, 224–225; Jackson, *Negro Office-Holders in Virginia*, 45–46.

[18] This is the contention of Morton, *Negro in Virginia Politics*, 128–129, 136–137, based upon "contemporary evidence of all kinds." Contemporary evidence on that subject is notably unreliable.

calling a convention to amend the Underwood Constitution. Article XII of that constitution stated that at the end of twenty years, in 1888, and at any time thereafter the legislature should decide, the question, "Shall there be a convention to revise the Constitution and amend the same," should be submitted to the people. In 1888, as was to be the case in 1897 (but not in 1900) the Democrats did not make the calling of a convention a party issue. The Republicans, though, generally opposed a convention.[19] The proposed convention was very little publicized or explained, and as a result many voted against it because they simply didn't know what it was all about.[20] On the Republican side, the Negroes wanted to retain the most liberal constitution the state has ever had and were not disposed to vote for a measure likely to lead to curtailing of their suffrage rights, while white Republicans of the West did not want to lose their Negro allies in the East. The white Democrats were still afraid of even the weakened power of Mahone and the possibility of a Mahone-dominated convention leading to an even more liberal constitution. Just as in 1897 and 1900, there were also entrenched political interests who feared the loss of their control. Probably most persuasive of all, however, as in 1897 and 1900, was the fact that it was not at all clear how to disfranchise the Negro without disfranchising many whites. White and black, Democrats and Republicans, thus combined to defeat the move for a convention.[21] The vote was exceedingly small, revealing the lack of interest in the allegedly "burning question" of controlling or eliminating the Negro voter. It was also exceedingly one-sided—63,125 votes opposing a convention and 3,698 for a convention. In the presidential election of the same year on the same day, the total Virginia vote was 301,519. The next year (1889) the total vote for governor was 284,028.[22]

     In his last serious bid for power, Mahone had the state Republican

---

[19] Ralph Clipman McDanel, "The Virginia Constitutional Convention of 1901–1902," *Johns Hopkins University Studies in Historical and Political Science,* XLVI (1928), 10.

[20] Jacob N. Brenaman, *A History of Virginia Conventions* (Richmond, Virginia, 1902), 81.

[21] Albert O. Porter, *County Government in Virginia: A Legislative History, 1607–1904, Columbia University Studies in History, Economics, and Public Law,* 526 (New York, 1947), 304–305; Writers' Program of the WPA, *Negro in Virginia,* 238.

[22] McDanel, "Virginia Constitutional Convention of 1901–1902," *Johns Hopkins University Studies in Historical and Political Science,* XLVI, p. 10; *Appletons' Annual Cyclopedia* (1889), 820.

convention nominate him for governor in 1889. One-hundred of the 600 participating delegates were Negroes,[23] and the majority of the Negro voters remained true to Mahone in spite of his bitter opposition to Langston the previous year. But Mahone's dictatorial and arrogant manner had alienated the last of his chief lieutenants, among them John S. Wise, former Readjuster Governor William E. Cameron, and John F. Lewis. When these men and a faction of some two-hundred followers met in convention and declared that, "The defeat of William Mahone is essential to the salvation of the [Virginia] Republican party," Mahone's defeat was indeed assured.[24] Also, his violent opposition to Langston had cost him greatly in Negro support. He was accused, with justice, of allowing no colored man "to gain and maintain prominence." Many colored men were reported determined to defeat him if they had "to elect a Democratic Governor by a solid Negro vote." It was reported that at a Mahone conference in Petersburg in July, 1888, to which a few Negroes were invited, they "were not allowed in the parlors of the house, but kept by themselves in a downstairs room." [25] Mahone himself said of the Negroes in the Republican party in 1889: "They have been made to understand that they must take a back seat and let their white bosses and political masters run the machine and have all the offices." [26]

Running against Mahone was a genial, likable Democrat named Philip W. McKinney. Although he had been in the middle of political struggles throughout the 1880's, he had not made himself offensive to the Republicans.[27] Thus it was not surprising that out of a total vote of 284,000, Mahone was defeated by about 42,000 votes.[28]

In the same election, the Democratic majority in the General Assembly was further increased. There remained but one Negro in the Senate—elected in 1887—and four Negro Delegates in the House. In all there were but twenty-four Republicans.[29] Two years later, in 1891, for the first time since Virginia rejoined the Union, no Negroes were elected to sit in the nation's oldest, representative as-

---

23 Eckenrode, "History of Virginia Since 1865," p. 229.
24 Morton, *Negro in Virginia Politics*, 129.
25 Clipping from New York *Sun*, July 17, 1889. Virginius D. Groner Political Scrapbook, 1888–1889 (Hampton Institute Library, Hampton, Virginia).
26 Quoted in Eckenrode, "History of Virginia Since 1865," p. 228.
27 Pendleton, *History of Appalachian Virginia*, 371–372.
28 *Appletons' Annual Cyclopedia* (1889), 820.
29 Morton, *Negro in Virginia Politics*, 130.

sembly.[30] Even more significant, though, was the fact that only three Republicans were left in the entire General Assembly.[31] Gone was not only the Mahone era, but two-party government as well. The Democratic party was in complete control. Its leadership were veterans in dealing with popular insurgent movements, and they had little trouble in out-maneuvering the Populist revolt which soon filled the void left by the demise of the state Republican party. These facts were far more significant in assuring one-party control than were any lessons "taught the Democrats" by the supporters of Mahone and by the little general himself. In spite of claims to the contrary, it cannot validly be said that, "The fraud and corruption practiced by Mahone and his followers to secure the dominance of their party taught the Democrats how to exclude the negro from participation in politics." [32] Before the Readjusters even appeared on the scene, the Democrats, then known as Conservatives, had, by means of the poll tax, congressional reapportionment, the whipping post, disfranchisement for *petit* larceny conviction, and listing of voters by race, virtually disfranchised the Negro through a smoothly working system "too complete to require any violence." [33] In 1883 and subsequently, outright intimidation,[34] congressional reapportionment, curbing of the power of local government, and especially the Anderson-McCormick election law—all these accomplished disfranchisement of the Negro.[35] The Democratic party needed no tutor in the art or science of disfranchisement. Cries such as, "And now for the fight this fall! We must beat the 'niggers' and their allies," [36] were sufficient enough to convince the average white man that his best interests lay with the Democratic party. Whether or not this was true was irrelevant. What was important was that the white voter be kept convinced that the Republican party was inescapably tied to "Negro rule." And such statements as the follow-

[30] Jackson, *Negro Office-Holders in Virginia*, p. VII.

[31] Morton, *Negro in Virginia Politics*, 131.

[32] McDanel, "Virginia Constitutional Convention of 1901–1902," *Johns Hopkins University Studies in Historical and Political Science*, XLVI, p. 8.

[33] Riddleberger, "Bourbonism in Virginia," *North American Review*, CXXXIV (1882), 425.

[34] For 1883, see "Election Frauds" subfolder of Mahone Papers, November 21–30, 1883.

[35] Morton, *Negro in Virginia Politics*, 123; Martin, "Negro Disfranchisement in Virginia," *Howard University Studies in the Social Sciences*, I, pp. 99–100.

[36] J. A. R. Varner to John Randolph Tucker, May 5, 1889. Tucker Family Papers (University of North Carolina Library).

ing further aided in keeping the white man in the "white man's party":

> There is a growing disinclination on the part of the white people to tax themselves for the education of an alien, [sic] non-tax-paying race, which is a willing instrument, at elections, in the hands of those who are regarded as the worst enemies of the South.[37]

In reality, the Negro was little more than a pawn or political football to be used, bribed, and cheated, and then sacrificed by *both* major political parties. In March, 1890, Edmund Randolph Cocke, Populist candidate for governor in 1893, but then a Democrat, wrote to Congressman H. St. George Tucker:

> The negro here [Cumberland county] is as free and has the same rights and privileges that I or any white man has. He votes as fearlessly and his vote is as honestly counted as mine or that of any other white man. I state what I know that our elections here are conducted with absolute fairness and honesty to all parties.[38]

Less than a year later Cocke wrote to Tucker:

> I have thought for some days that if Senator [Benjamin F.] Butler [Massachusetts] would only introduce his proposition for the repeal of the XV Amendment depriving the negro of suffrage that it might have a good effect. If you think it will do so please suggest it . . . some Republicans are in favor of it . . . . the only solution to prevent troubles . . . [is] to disfranchise the negro.[39]

Two years later Cocke and the Populist party sought to dissociate themselves from the Negro vote by not seeking it and by attempting to dispel the popular belief that they were.[40]

Populism was a grass-roots revolt of Southern and Western farmers bowed down by low prices for their crops, high prices for what they bought, scarcity of cash and credit, and the power of monopolies such as the railroads. The Populist party should have provided the perfect framework for a political alliance along economic and class lines, rather than racial lines. And in the South generally it did

---

[37] J. L. M. Curry to R. C. Winthrop, March 25, 1890. Curry Papers.

[38] Edmund Randolph Cocke to H. St. George Tucker, March 14, 1890. Tucker Family Papers.

[39] *Ibid.*, January 25, 1891.

[40] Helen M. Blackburn, "The Populist Party in the South, 1890–1898," Unpublished M. A. Thesis (Howard University, 1941), 45.

provide it, especially in South Carolina, Georgia, and Texas. The Virginia Negro, too, tended to support Populist candidates, but he did so in the absence of strong Republican candidates and out of opposition to those of the Democratic party, which, in his eyes was the symbol of his oppression.[41]

The value of the Negro vote was not lost on Virginia's white Populist leaders, but neither was the fact that Negro support of a party always branded it as "the party of the Negro." That designation had not only discredited thoroughly respectable Republicanism in Virginia, it had also been a major factor in the defeat of Virginia's most recent upsurge of liberalism—that of Mahone and the Readjusters. Crude but effective propaganda by the Democratic party and the Democratic press always succeeded in discrediting any movement which had the support of the Negro. Besides, the Populist party of Virginia had the distinction of being led by gentlemen—by disgruntled, liberal-minded Democrats of social and economic standing—but men whose liberalism did not include political equality for the Negro.

The small white farmer of Virginia knew that he had far more in common with the Negro farmer than he did with the ruling element of the Democratic party, the opponent of Populism. Both the Negro and the white farmer were caught in the same economic vise which gave rise to Populism. But the white farmers who might have supported the Populist or People's party were undoubtedly greatly reduced in number by such political tactics as those used by Colonel Thomas Smith of Warrenton, at the Sixth District Democratic Convention of 1892. Said Smith: "The man blessed with a white cuticle is false if he does not in this emergency [the Populist revolt] cooperate with the Democratic Party." [42] Said Sheldon, "The election of 1892 made apparent once more the fact that economic issues must remain subordinate to the racial problem in the South so long as the negro was a potential fact in politics." [43] At the Virginia Populist party convention that year, not a Negro was present.[44] Still

---

[41] William DuBose Sheldon, *Populism in the Old Dominion: Virginia Farm Politics, 1885–1900* (Princeton, N. J., 1935), 90.
[42] Quoted in Sheldon, *Populism in the Old Dominion*, 87–88 from the Richmond *Dispatch*, August 25, 1892.
[43] *Ibid.*, 92.
[44] Blackburn, "Populist Party in the South," M. A. Thesis (Howard University, 1941), 45.

there was no place else for the Negro to go. After the election of 1891, only three Republicans, none of them Negroes, were left in the General Assembly.[45] Thus it was not surprising that, in 1893, the Republicans made no nominations for either the gubernatorial office or the General Assembly.[46]

In the Populist party, the Democrats had their only significant opposition, and around that standard both white and black Republicans rallied in a fusion of parties which gave Cocke, the Populist candidate for governor, 81,239 votes, to 127,940 for Charles T. O'Ferrall the Democrat, and 2,777 for J. R. Miller the Prohibitionist.[47] In all likelihood, though, it was the white Republican vote rather than that of the Negroes which swelled the Populist total to more than two-thirds that of the Democrats. The *Rockingham Register* estimated that only about a third of the eligible Negro voters actually cast their votes and that one-fifth of the Negro vote cast was for the Democratic ticket.[48] In support of this statement, the Negro Democratic League had voted in October to support the Democratic ticket on the grounds that it was to their best interest to vote with "that class of white people that own and control everything." Their resolution further admitted that the white people could a thousand times more readily afford to dispense with their labor than they could afford to do without the compensation paid them.[49] Here indeed was political despair speaking through the voice of economic expediency. It is not surprising then that with the Republican party a virtual nullity and Negroes' support unsolicited and discouraged by the Populists,[50] large numbers of Negroes turned to the Democrats in furtherance of what appeared to be their best interests.

With the Negro vote no longer a threat to Democratic party control —the Anderson-McCormick election law having done its work—the

---

[45] Morton, *Negro in Virginia Politics*, 131.

[46] *Ibid.*, 131.

[47] *Warrock-Richardson Almanack* (1895), 66.

[48] Cited in Charles E. Wynes, "Charles T. O'Ferrall and the Virginia Gubernatorial Election of 1893," *Virginia Magazine of History and Biography*, LXIV (October, 1956), 451, from the Harrisonburg *Rockingham Register*, November 17, 1893.

[49] Lynchburg *Daily Advance*, October 10, 1893.

[50] In 1894, a writer in the Populist organ, the *Virginia Sun*, began an essay on the rights of the Negro with the statement, "This is a white man's country and will always be controlled by the whites." Richmond *Virginia Sun*, December 20, 1894.

Democrats decided that a new election law was needed. This one was to clean up general fraud and corruption, whereby in some areas even white Democrats were bidding against one another in the purchase of Negro votes. Defeat of Mahone and the Readjusters in 1883 had put the Virginia Negro on the road to disfranchisement. The Populist revolt was little more than an interval in which an incipient economic alliance across racial lines was quashed by a most politically respectable, white leadership which discouraged and disowned Negro support. This policy bespoke not so much racial prejudice as it did knowledge of the fact that Negro support of a party made it the "party of the Negro"—a sure kiss of death. And there was the example of the Republican party to prove it. And beyond this, white Virginians had not forgotten the "nightmare of Mahone and Negro rule"—a nightmare largely created by Democratic politicians and a Democratic press.

Chapter 4

Disfranchisement, 1894–1902

AS THE decade of the 1890's wore on, the Negro increasingly became a mere irritant in Virginia politics. Republicanism no longer posed a threat to Democratic party rule. And the Negro, aware that the Republican party which had forsaken him was now itself impotent, increasingly turned to the expediency of "accommodation" and sold his vote to the Democrat who offered the highest price. By 1894, the Negro had seen his vote become a commodity to be bought and sold like any other.[1] Political corruption in Virginia had become so general that it was a source of embarrassment, as newspapers within and without the state commented on its extent. Thus it was with the view of cleaning up the elections that a modified disfranchising law based on literacy was passed in 1894. This law was the Walton Act, which, like its predecessor, the Anderson-McCormick law, kept the election machinery firmly in the hands of the Democratic party. It also provided for a ballot which required some degree of literacy for proper marking.

Ironically, the Walton Act was also a product of the Valley, where Negroes were a tiny minority. Its author was Senator M. L. Walton of Page and Shenandoah counties, where the Negro population was about ten and three percent respectively. This fact is indicative of the extent of election frauds, even in overwhelmingly white and predominantly Republican areas. The Democrats had no monopoly on unethical election practices, for, given the opportunity, the Republicans could be as corrupt as were the Democrats, even among themselves.[2]

The Walton Act provided for the use of ballots which contained no symbols or other party designations. Voters secretly marked their choices in the privacy of polling booths, but anyone who could not read the names could request the assistance of a specially appointed constable to assist him. Over half of Virginia's Negro population was

---

[1] Morton, *Negro in Virginia Politics*, 133.

[2] McDanel, "Virginia Constitutional Convention of 1901–1902," *Johns Hopkins University Studies in Histrical and Political Science*, XLVI, pp. 31–32; Herman L. Horn, "The Growth and Development of the Democratic Party in Virginia Since 1890," Unpublished Ph.D. Dissertation (Duke University, 1949), 45–46.

illiterate, as were a considerable portion of the whites. Embarrassed by their ignorance and ashamed to admit it, vast numbers of the illiterate stayed away from the polls, marked the wrong candidate, or marked the ballot in such a manner that it was thrown out. Besides, there was nothing to prevent the special constable from indicating the wrong candidate to the illiterate who asked for assistance. Local Democratic election boards provided for by the Anderson-Mc-Cormick law were retained by the Walton Act. They in turn appointed three election judges, one of whom was supposed to be a representative of the minority party. But another provision of the act stipulated that no election could be held invalid because all three election judges were members of the same party. As was intended, the Walton Act disfranchised many of the illiterate, but it was so written that the illiterate who slipped through, by requesting assistance from the special constable, *could* have their votes nullified or mis-cast as a result of that constable's being a friend of the election judges. So susceptible to fraud was this part of the new law that, in 1896, at the instance of its original sponsor, the Walton Act was amended; the special constable was eliminated, his duties to be filled by one of the election judges chosen by themselves. It is not at all clear, however, how this increased the honesty of elections if the appointed judge was prone to take advantage of the opportunity for fraud thereby presented. At the same time, the act was amended so that the candidates' names appeared in the same order and in Roman type on all ballots.[3] The type of print was stipulated, because, in 1894 and 1895 in the Tenth District, comprising several Valley counties where many persons still spoke and read German, both Negroes and Democrats of Anglo-Saxon extraction were discriminated against through resort to ballots printed in German text and/or script, type.[4]

There is no evidence that the Walton Act, even after being amended, substantially increased the honesty of elections. But the disfranchisement of large numbers of the illiterate and the use of the secret ballot in closed polling booths produced a greater *appearance* of honesty.

In 1895, shortly before his death, Mahone called a meeting in Petersburg to organize a campaign for honest elections. The Popu-

---

[3] Pendleton, *History of Appalachian Virginia*, 374–376; Morton, *Negro in Virginia Politics*, 133 and 133 n.

[4] Pendleton, *History of Appalachian Virginia*, 402–403.

lists, who were also agitating for a non-partisan election law,[5] sent a number of their leading members to the Mahone meeting, thereby confirming many people's belief that Populism, Mahoneism, and the Negroes were all bound up together.[6]

Not only were Negroes not allowed to vote, they often were not allowed to register. When a number of ranking state Democrats, rapidly falling out with the free silver advocates, demanded that Negroes be registered and voted in the presidential election of 1896, the Richmond *Dispatch* charged them with attempting to "negrofy" Virginia by paving the way to turn the state over to them in 1897.[7] Such statements were, of course, rank demagoguery. They were aimed specifically at Governor O'Ferrall himself, Congressman G. O. Wise, Judge John T. Goolrick, and Richmond City Attorney, C. V. Meredith. In 1897, Governor O'Ferrall denounced before the General Assembly the chronic fraud in Virginia elections.[8] And already the anomaly had been noted of the Democrats' receiving their heaviest majorities where the Negro population was greatest.[9]

The Walton Act, no less than the Anderson-McCormick election law, was a white man's law; and no less did it operate to assure Democratic supremacy. It had indeed eliminated many of the so-called undesirable voters, but like its predecessor, it made a farce of honest elections. At any rate, "The white people of Virginia had practically disfranchised the negroes by the middle of the nineties. . . ." [10]

The Negro increasingly lost all hope of advancing himself either socially or politically, and as he lost hope he evinced less and less interest in the larger political issues. In 1896, when silver was the issue, the Virginia Negro took little part in the national election.[11] By 1899, the Negro bothered to vote only in local elections.[12] Democratic county chairmen admonished the precinct chairmen even in the Valley, "Watch the Colored new registration. See your Registrar and

[5] *Ibid.*, 395–396.
[6] Horn, "Growth and Development of the Democratic Party in Virginia Since 1890," Ph.D. Dissertation (Duke University, 1949), 40.
[7] Cited in Allen Wesley Moger, *The Rebuilding of the Old Dominion: A Study in Economic, Social, and Political Transition from 1880 to 1912* (Ann Arbor, Michigan, 1940), 34.
[8] Pendleton, *History of Appalachian Virginia*, 400.
[9] *Ibid.*, 394.
[10] Morton, *Negro in Virginia Politics*, 134.
[11] Eckenrode, "History of Virginia Since 1865," pp. 274–275.
[12] *Ibid.*, 276.

have him question these applicants closely." [13] By the year 1900, the Negro had become such a manageable political force that J. W. Bryant could write from Crewe to J. M. Harris, district Democratic chairman, that for eight or ten dollars he could hire twenty-five to fifty Negroes to hiss a Republican opponent off the speaker's platform at the courthouse in Nottoway county. [14] Another correspondent wrote to Harris: "[H. H.] Dyson says he does not intend to allow the negors [sic] to vote at the ballot box in Nottoway CH (all that he can control.)" [15]

Thus it could truthfully be said by the end of the century, that,

Thirty years after . . . [the adoption of the Fifteenth Amendment] the negro race has less [sic] political rights than it had then. Today, the negro has no political right which the white man feels called upon to respect, if that right involves in the slightest degree the possibility of negro domination or even political equality. [16]

Sentiment in favor of outright disfranchisement of the Negro by legal means was growing, and in 1897 the question of a constitutional convention was again raised. As in 1888, the matter appeared to have been aired only to test the political wind, because the Democrats did not make it a party issue in spite of the fact that the Republicans generally opposed it. The Negro Protective Association also opposed a convention—on economic grounds. The Association—and many white people—argued that the state was too poor to spend so much money unnecessarily. Virginia was still feeling the results of the Panic of 1893 and of the severe weather and bad crops which had accompanied it. The Association also declared that a constitutional convention could make little if any further progress toward disfranchising the Negro. [17] Most white people knew this was so, and if the reason for calling a convention was only to clean up the

---

[13] W. T. McCue, Chairman of the Augusta County Democratic Committee, in a form letter to Augusta county precinct chairmen, September 16, 1897. McCue Family Papers (University of Virginia Library).

[14] J. W. Bryant to J. M. Harris, October 2, 1900. Eppes-Kilmartin Papers (University of Virginia Library).

[15] C. E. Downs to J. M. Harris, October 22, 1900. Eppes-Kilmartin Papers.

[16] Alsen F. Thomas, *The Virginia Constitutional Convention and its Possibilities* (Lynchburg, Virginia, 1901), 16.

[17] Proceedings of the Negro Protective Association, May 18, 1897, p. 3. Luther P. Jackson Papers (Virginia State College Library). On disfranchisement of the Negro by the mid-1890's see Morton, *Negro in Virginia Politics*, 134; Eckenrode, "History of Virginia Since 1865," pp. 274–276; Thomas, *Virginia Constitutional Convention and its Possibilities*, 16.

elections, then the size of the vote did not indicate that the mass of Virginians were greatly concerned about election frauds. Little publicity had been given to the matter, and when the people went to the polls to decide the question, the result was an overwhelming defeat of the proposed convention. The vote was 83,435 against and 38,326 for a convention.[18] The total vote was thus only 121,761, while in the same year the total vote in one of the dullest gubernatorial contests on record was 166,495. In the presidential election of the previous year, in which few Negroes voted, the total vote was 294,841.[19]

The vote, however, did reveal growing interest in and sentiment for a convention. In 1888, when the convention question was last voted upon, the vote had been a one-sided 63,125 against, to 3,698 for a convention.[20] There is no evidence whatever that public sentiment made a constitutional convention mandatory. But there were factors which made a convention appear desirable to many Democratic leaders. At least one of them was very practical. Virginia elections had become so fraudulent that, although the Democratic party safely dominated the state, that party could never be sure that a Republican Congress would not refuse to seat Virginia Representatives on grounds of fraud or throwing out of the Negro vote. Between 1874 and 1900, there took place twenty such contested Virginia elections, sixteen of which involved fraud and four either interpretation of the Walton Act or eligibility of one of the contestants.[21] Of the extent of fraud one investigator has written:

> Probably at no time in the history of the state have election frauds been so openly practiced as during the years between 1870 and 1902. . . . While the politicians of the Tidewater were able to advance the cause of "white supremacy" as a moral [*sic*] justification for chicanery, there was no such excuse in the Western areas of the state, where the colored population was negligible; but there were as many frauds in the Mountains as in the East, though here they were often practiced by the Republicans at the expense of the Democrats [or of other Republicans].[22]

---

[18] McDanel, "Virginia Constitutional Convention of 1901–1902," *Johns Hopkins University Studies in Historical and Political Science*, XLVI, p. 10; Brenaman, *History of Virginia Conventions*, 82.

[19] *Warrock-Richardson Almanack* (1902), 65.

[20] *Appletons' Annual Cyclopedia* (1889), 820.

[21] McDanel, "Virginia Constitutional Convention of 1901–1902," *Johns Hopkins University Studies in Historical and Political Science*, XLVI, p. 11.

[22] Porter, *County Government in Virginia*, 304.

Thus, a thoroughly commendable moral reason urged the holding of a constitutional convention, even though this reason involved resort to Machiavellian means. Many people, including some Republicans, sincerely desired to clean up Virginia elections by the most direct means—disfranchisement of the Negro legally so that white people would not have to cheat and defraud him illegally.[23] In the western portion of the state, where the Negro was of no political significance but where fraud and corruption were also widespread,[24] disfranchisement would supposedly result in a general reduction of the electorate and removal from the voter registration books of the rowdier, poor, mountain whites. The fallacy in the scheme to get honest elections by resort to legal disfranchisement was, of course, that it sacrificed politically the injured party—the very ones who were being bought, used, defrauded, and cheated out of their constitutional rights.

To those who advocated a convention, 1900 seemed a propitious time. Mahone and Mahoneism were dead; Populism had ceased to be a threat; the disruptive silver issue had passed from the scene; and the Negro as a voter no longer constituted a threat anywhere in the state. Besides, the Virginia Republican party was split in many directions. In 1899, there was so much dissension in its ranks that in only a few districts were there Republican candidates for seats in the General Assembly.[25] And finally, there was the fact that, in 1898, in the case of *Williams vs. Mississippi*, the United States Supreme Court had upheld the constitutionality of just such a disfranchising constitution as many of Virginia's Democratic leaders had in mind.

Aside from the lack of publicity and of general interest, there had been another reason for failure of convention attempts in 1888 and 1897. Those attempts had been led by a small group of independents who had never reconciled themselves to the Underwood Constitution of 1869. In the year 1900, once again the move was led by Democrats of the antimachine faction—men who were no special

[23] McDanel, "Virginia Constitutional Convention of 1901–1902," *Johns Hopkins University Studies in Historical and Political Science,* XLVI, p. 33.

[24] *Ibid.,* 31–32; Porter, *County Government in Virginia,* 304; Horn, "Growth and Development of the Democratic Party in Virginia Since 1890," Ph.D. Dissertation (Duke University, 1949), 45–46.

[25] Horn, "Growth and Development of the Democratic Party in Virginia Since 1890," Ph.D. Dissertation (Duke University, 1949), 43, 49; Writers Program of the WPA, *Negro in Virginia,* 238; Richmond *Twice A Week Times,* February 6, 1900; Pendleton, *History of Appalachian Virginia,* 418.

friends of the machine boss, Thomas Staples Martin. An Albemarle county lawyer, Martin was unknown to most Virginians until 1893, when, by judicious personal use of certain railroad contributions to the Democratic party, he had, to nearly everyone's amazement, succeeded not only to the late John S. Barbour's seat in the U. S. Senate, but to the position of state Democratic machine leader as well.[26] The independents, led by William A. Jones, Carter Glass, William A. Anderson (co-author of the Anderson-McCormick election law of 1884), Andrew Jackson Montague, and Eugene Withers argued not only for election reforms, but for reduction of the number of state, county, and municipal offices created by the Underwood Constitution.[27] On the other hand, many Democratic officeholders opposed the convention on the very practical grounds that they might find their offices swept away. Senator Martin, the boss of the machine, kept silent, supposedly in opposition. At the same time he and the machine retained their maneuverability by not actively opposing a convention. Outwardly, at least, the Democratic party maintained a united front and an appearance of harmony.[28]

On March 5, 1900, the legislature passed an act calling for a referendum on the question of a convention. The referendum was set for May 24, less than three months away. This time, the Democrats made the convention a party issue, so that Democrats would either vote for it or not at all.[29] They were aided in doing this by the bulk of the Republicans, who generally opposed a convention. There were some Republicans of the lily-white faction, however, who favored a convention and disfranchisement of the Negro on the grounds that only by removal of the colored voter from Republican ranks could that party make itself respectable in the eyes of the mass of white Virginians.[30]

Actually, the only real desire to disfranchise the Negro existed in counties where he might allegedly threaten white control because

---

[26] On Martin, see James A. Bear, Jr., "Thomas Staples Martin: A Study in Virginia Politics, 1893–1896," Unpublished M. A. Thesis (University of Virginia, 1952).

[27] Pendleton, *History of Appalachian Virginia*, 439–440.

[28] *Ibid.*, 440; McDanel, "Virginia Constitutional Convention of 1901–1902," *Johns Hopkins University Studies in Historical and Political Science*, XLVI, pp. 13–15.

[29] Horn, "Growth and Development of the Democratic Party in Virginia Since 1890," Ph.D. Dissertation (Duke University, 1949), 51.

[30] *Ibid.*, 58.

of his numbers, or where he furnished the excuse for election frauds.[31] Even there, it was not at all clear how any constitutional provision which would disfranchise the black man would not also at least make possible disfranchisement of the poor whites. Many Virginians, white and colored, again objected to the cost of a convention as they had in 1897. By 1900, Virginia was just beginning to taste of good times again.[32] The pro-convention argument of "too many government offices" was therefore brought forth to sway the economy-minded.

The smallness of the vote indicated that there was no great general interest in disfranchising the Negro or in reducing the number of government offices. The total vote was only 137,737, with 77,362 votes for the convention and 60,375 against. The following November (1900) the total state vote for President was 264,095, with the vote for Bryan, the Democrat, alone exceeding the total vote on the convention by more than 8,000. In the vote for governor in November, 1901, the total vote was 198,048.[33] In 1897, when the question of a convention was not a party issue and when it was not publicized, the total vote was only 15,976 votes smaller. Then the vote was 83,435 against a convention and 38,326 for one.[34]

An analysis of the vote reveals that the convention was brought about by the votes of the black counties and the cities, as opposed to the white counties. This was so because the Negroes were discouraged from voting and because their votes when cast often were mis-counted or thrown out altogether.[35]

The Southwest, with the smallest percentage of Negro population in the state, voted solidly against the convention, with the exception of Giles county. Opposition was also strong in the Valley, but exactly half of the counties there favored the convention. The Piedmont was the area which consistently favored the convention. In the counties which had more Negroes than whites, the vote was the most striking. There were thirty-five such counties, seventeen of which favored the convention, while eighteen opposed it.

---

[31] McDanel, "Virginia Constitutional Convention of 1901–1902," *Johns Hopkins University Studies in Historical and Political Science,* XLVI, p. 18.
[32] Eckenrode, "History of Virginia Since 1865," p. 283.
[33] *Warrock-Richardson Almanack* (1903), 50.
[34] Brenaman, *History of Virginia Conventions,* 82.
[35] McDanel, "Virginia Constitutional Convention of 1901–1902," *Johns Hopkins University Studies in Historical and Political Science,* XLVI, p. 18.

In all, forty-eight counties favored the convention and fifty-two opposed it. Of the sixty-five counties with a predominantly white population, thirty favored the convention and thirty-five opposed it. All of the cities were in favor of it.

The counties with less than fifty percent Negro population were not preeminently concerned with disfranchising the Negro, and hence more than half of them opposed the convention.[36] Disfranchisement there too often meant sacrificing the votes of poor whites. Many of these counties also had strong Republican affiliations, and that party was less willing than the eastern Democrats to sacrifice its poor whites, out of necessity if not always out of principle. Besides, the matter of a convention had been made a party issue, and parties in Virginia were largely a reflection of the old sectional antagonism.

In the counties with black majorities, most of the whites who voted apparently desired to put an end to the Negro vote. That they could do so in the face of a black numerical majority was due to the fact that the Negro in practice had already been disfranchised[37] and few bothered even to attempt to vote. Negroes whose votes had not been purchased by the Democrats often had their ballots thrown out or counted otherwise than as cast. The Petersburg *Index-Appeal* of May 25, 1900, claimed that the Negro vote in both Petersburg and in the state at large was against the convention, but that it was not so counted.[38]

The very style in which the ballots were printed made the election grossly unfair to those who opposed a convention. They bore only the words, "For Constitutional Convention." Unmarked ballots were counted "for"; hence, those who favored a convention had only to pick up their ballots and drop them in the ballot box without even entering the polling booths. Those who wished to vote against a convention had to enter the polling booth, perhaps request the assistance of the appointed election judge, and mark through all three words printed on the ballot. If any word remained unmarked through, or if anything else was written on the ballot, it was

---

[36] *Ibid.*, 18; Morton, *Negro in Virginia Politics*, 148–150; Pendleton, *History of Appalachian Virginia*, 443.

[37] Morton, *Negro in Virginia Politics*, 134; Eckenrode, "History of Virginia Since 1865," pp. 274–276; Thomas, *Virginia Constitutional Convention and Its Possibilities*, 16.

[38] Cited in Horn, "Growth and Development of the Democratic Party in Virginia Since 1890," Ph.D. Dissertation (Duke University, 1949), 61.

thrown out as mutilated.[39] Where white sentiment was known to be pro-convention, neither poor white nor Negro was likely to make himself so conspicuous as to enter a polling booth to cross out the ballot. It was easier simply not to vote.

Governor Tyler proceeded to call a special session of the legislature for January 23, 1901, to work out plans for the selection of convention delegates. The special session met, and on February 16, 1901, it passed an act calling for the selection of one-hundred delegates to be elected on the basis of representation in the House of Delegates.[40] The act providing for selection of the delegates also included the Democratic party pledge that any new proposed constitution which emerged from the convention would be submitted to the people for ratification or rejection.[41]

The convention of eighty-eight Democrats and twelve Republicans met on June 12, 1901, and the former Populist but now once again Democrat, John Goode of Bedford, was elected president. There was much fretting throughout the state, even from conservative newspapers, before chairman John W. Daniel's Committee on the Election Franchise presented a majority and a minority report to the convention in late September. They were ordered to be laid on the table.[42] There is evidence that Daniel, who was not among those demanding a convention, had major reservations about disfranchising the Negro. Walter A. Watson, convention delegate from Nottoway and Amelia counties, recorded in his diary during the convention that Daniel was not willing to do anything effective toward the Negro suffrage question. Watson said Daniel's sympathy did not embrace the white people of the so-called black counties. Said Watson: "He discussed the race question with me and thinks the negro race will never be mixed with the white. Wish I felt as sure."[43]

In October, 1901, the Democratic conference within the convention

---

[39] Pendleton, *History of Appalachian Virginia*, 440–441.

[40] David L. Pulliam, *The Constitutional Conventions of Virginia from the Foundation of the Commonwealth to the Present Time* (Richmond, Virginia, 1901), 154–157.

[41] *Report of the Proceedings and Debates of the Constitutional Convention, State of Virginia, 1901–1902* (Richmond, Virginia, 1906), I, p. 99.

[42] McDanel, "Virginia Constitutional Convention of 1901–1902," *Johns Hopkins University Studies in Historical and Political Science*, XLVI, pp. 38–39.

[43] Walter A. Watson, *Notes on Southside Virginia*, edited by Mrs. Walter A. Watson, *Bulletin of the Virginia State Library* (Richmond, Virginia, September, 1925), XV, p. 213.

briefly discussed the reports of the Committee on the Elective Franchise, but not until March 8, 1902, did that conference really get down to discussing them seriously. From March 8th to the 29th, the convention daily adjourned immediately after roll-call in order to allow the Democratic members to give their full attention to the suffrage question in closed party conference, where no records were kept. On March 31, the Democrats reported to the convention a proposed election article which they largely agreed upon, and the only debate on the crucial suffrage question in the convention at large, where records were kept, took place between March 31 and April 4, 1902.[44]

Defense of the principle of manhood suffrage was generally left to the twelve Republican convention delegates. With no Negro problem in the West, they were not nearly so concerned over the question of disfranchisement as were the delegates from the East. Allen Caperton Braxton, Democratic delegate from Augusta county and the city of Staunton in the Valley, declared to the convention that that section of the state was more interested in economic reform—especially control of the railroads—than it was in the Negro question, which was no real concern there anyway.[45] In essence, the Valley and the West were demanding economic reforms in return for supporting Eastern schemes for curbing the suffrage. It was no accident that Braxton was made chairman of the Committee on Corporations. And it was from that committee's report that there emerged the powerful State Corporation Commission, which gave the state, after 1902, almost dictatorial power over corporations which operated within it.

While some delegates sincerely believed that they were convened to consider all of Virginia's problems which came within the purview of a constitutional convention, others, like Carter Glass and the forthright A. P. Thom of Norfolk, believed that it was purely and simply a disfranchising convention. Asked Thom: "If you are not to disfranchise our black men, why are we here?"[46] William G. Robertson, a Democrat representing Craig and Roanoke counties and the city of Roanoke, had a higher regard for the convention and why it was called. Robertson maintained that,

[44] *Proceedings and Debates of the Constitutional Convention of 1901–1902*, II, pp. 2937–3096.
[45] *Ibid.*, II, p. 2451.
[46] *Ibid.*, II, p. 2974.

They [*i.e.* those who voted for the convention] commissioned us to come here and sit, in Convention assembled, to decide what was for the best and highest interests of this Commonwealth. There was no particular question, whether connected with the suffrage or economical, that we came here to consider.[47]

Robertson's statesmanlike view was admirable, but in reality, the 77,362 Virginians who had voted for a convention—minus those whose votes had been fraudulently counted "for"—had quite probably voted for a convention to disfranchise the Negro.

It was true, however, that white Virginians were extremely reluctant to approve the calling of a constitutional convention which might rob numbers of them, as well as the Negroes, of their franchise. The convention of 1901–1902 was not the result of public demand. Whatever its faults, the Underwood Constitution satisfied the mass of white Virginians, and the Negroes were not going to vote for a convention plainly aimed at disfranchising them.[48] Robert W. Blair, Republican delegate from Wythe county, reminded the convention:

It is useless . . . to contend that the white people of this Commonwealth demanded a Constitutional Convention. The proposition had been continuously agitated by the politicians of this State for the last fifteen years.[49]

Delegates in the convention freely admitted that white Virginians who knew the true political condition of the state no longer had any fears of Negro domination, as they had had from 1870 to 1884. What they feared was the Negro's very presence and the way in which he might be used by unscrupulous politicians of both parties.[50] Or, put more directly, in the words of A. P. Gillespie, Republican delegate from Tazewell county, what was really meant was that "the Negro vote of this Commonwealth must be destroyed to prevent the Democratic election officers [provided for by the Anderson-McCormick law and kept by the Walton Act] from stealing their votes. . . ."[51]

[47] *Ibid.*, II, p. 2992.
[48] Writers Program of the WPA, *Negro in Virginia*, 238.
[49] *Proceedings and Debates of the Constitutional Convention of 1901–1902*, II, p. 3119.
[50] *Ibid.*, Delegate A. P. Thom, II, p. 2961.
[51] *Ibid.*, II, p. 3014.

Deriding the Machiavellian claim that honest elections could take place only if certain of the voters were disfranchised, A. L. Pedigo, Republican delegate from Henry county, declared:

> The infamous election law [Walton Act] that now disgraces our statute books must be abated. Nearly all agree to this, but a part of our people who style themselves the best people contend that they cannot concede honest elections except on condition that a very large number of the voters be disfranchised. They well know they are in the minority. . . . They say the negro . . . has irritated them and caused them to sin. . . . I have heard the remark of late so often that the government of Virginia is a government of lawyers that I have come to fully believe it.[52] [Sixty-two of the one-hundred delegates to the convention had been trained in the law.] [53]

To Pedigo, "The best people . . . [of Virginia were] trying to take the government out of the hands of the common people and to organize a highly-paid aristocracy." [54]

Few could doubt that any measure which would disfranchise the Negro would also disfranchise at least some whites. Delegates like Norfolk's A. P. Thom, who openly announced their conviction that the convention had been called to disfranchise the Negro,[55] expressed fear that proposed measures such as capitation tax payment as a voting prerequisite would remove as many white voters as black ones.[56] Other delegates, like Richard McIlwaine, Democrat of Prince Edward county, forthrightly came out for excluding the illiterate and lower class of white men as well as black.[57] Many Southerners regarded disfranchisement of the Negro as a progressive reform. A smaller number, including scholars like Virginia's Philip Alexander Bruce, also regarded as a progressive reform the use of constitutional disfranchising clauses against the uneducated white man.[58] Moreover, those who advocated disfranchisement of

---

[52] *Ibid.*, II, p. 3049.
[53] McDanel, "Virginia Constitutional Convention of 1901–1902," *Johns Hopkins University Studies in Historical and Political Science*, XLVI, p. 20.
[54] *Proceedings and Debates of the Constitutional Convention of 1901–1902*, II, p. 3057. C. Vann Woodward, *Origins of the New South*, maintains that this motive was present in all the Southern states, p. 330.
[55] *Ibid.*, II, p. 2974.
[56] *Ibid.*, II, p. 2981.
[57] *Ibid.*, II, pp. 2998–3006.
[58] Philip Alexander Bruce, *The Rise of the New South*, vol. XVII of *The History of North America* (Philadelphia, 1905), 470–471.

the black man could hardly have failed to perceive that removal of the Negro voter would also mean removal of a special inducement for the white man to go to the polls—namely, that of outvoting the Negro.[59]

It was a foregone conclusion, however, that the new constitution would include a disfranchisement provision of some kind. But the people of Virginia thoroughly believed that whatever the product of the convention was, they would have a choice of accepting or rejecting it in a popular vote. The Democratic party had pledged that, and the General Assembly had provided for it by law.[60]

In order to calm the fears of those who were concerned that whatever provision disfranchised the Negro would also disfranchise many whites, the proposed franchise article liberally provided for registration of all persons *prior to January, 1904.* Until then, all might register who met stipulated and reasonable age and residence requirements, and who were also persons that either: (1) were veterans of the Civil War (Union or Confederate), (2) were sons of veterans, (3) owned property on which they had paid taxes of at least one dollar in the preceding year, (4) could read *and* explain, or if unable to read, explain when read to, any section of the new constitution. Virtually all white men could qualify under at least one of these provisions. Negroes could not qualify under either the veteran or son of a veteran provisions. Most of them did not own property on which they paid taxes, while many who owned property had neglected to pay the tax; so that provision did not aid them greatly either. And it was certain that few of them could read and/ or explain any part of the new constitution to the satisfaction of white, and usually Democratic, registrars.

It was the second part of the franchise article which represented the determination of many of the delegates to generally curb the suffrage. By it, all those who registered *after* January 1, 1904, in addition to meeting the usual age and residence requirements, had to have paid a poll tax of a dollar-and-a-half for each of the three preceeding years, *and*, unless *physically* unable, make written application in the presence of the registrar, stating stipulated personal,

[59] *Ibid.*, 450.
[60] *Proceedings and Debates of the Constitutional Convention of 1901–1902*, I, p. 99.

occupational, and past voting history, without benefit of any aid or suggestion. Finally, they had to answer under oath any and all questions which the registration officials chose to ask them about their qualifications as electors.[61] And to make sure that the poll tax did its work, it was further provided that payment should not be legally required prior to 1904, when three years' poll taxes would be due if one wished to register to vote. Thus, those who desired to register that year or after, unless they had just become twenty-one years of age, had to pay $4.50, not $1.50 for the right to vote.[62]

Both the franchise article and the constitution as a whole were overwhelmingly approved by the convention delegates. The only remaining question before the convention was whether to proclaim the constitution or submit it to a vote as promised and as required by the act authorizing the convention.[63] Disregarding the ethical obligation to submit the constitution to the people, the delegates argued for over a month whether they had ample legal precedent for proclaiming it. To their satisfaction they decided that they did. They were afraid to submit the constitution to the old electorate, because men just did not vote for their own disfranchisement. Ethically, it would have been too highhanded to submit it to the new electorate, although there was ample legal precedent for doing so. Both the Virginia constitution of 1830 and that of 1851 had been submitted to the new electorate. But in both cases the new electorate had been a greatly expanded one. Besides, the "understanding clause," under which ignorant white men might register till 1904, but by which any Negro could be rejected, was as patently fraudulent as the very practices which the convention had allegedly been called to remedy.

It was generally believed then, and was probably true, that had the new constitution been submitted to the people, it would have been defeated.[64] And, if there had been indication at the time of the convention referendum in May, 1900, that the pledge of the Democratic party and the act of the General Assembly requiring submis-

---

[61] *Virginia Constitution of 1902*, Article II, Sections 18–21.
[62] *Ibid.*, Article II, Section 22.
[63] *Proceedings and Debates of the Constitutional Convention of 1901–1902*, I, p. 99.
[64] McDanel, "Virginia Constitutional Convention of 1901–1902," *Johns Hopkins University Studies in Historical and Political Science*, XLVI, p. 129.

sion would not be honored, "the calling of the convention would probably have been defeated and the people would not have been so apathetic in regard to the convention." [65]

In 1904, when the permanent suffrage provisions went into effect, it became apparent how well the convention had done its work of reducing the electorate. The total state vote for President that year was only 129,929. In the previous presidential election of 1900, under the old constitution, but when few Negroes voted anyway, the total vote was 264,095. The voting electorate had been cut in half. In 1900, 147 votes were cast per thousand of the state's population; in 1904, only 67 votes per thousand were cast. [66] By 1940, aided by the primary election, among other factors, fewer than 10 Virginians per thousand were voting. [67]

With all danger of Republican rule and Negro rule of local areas removed, the democracy of the Democractic party was perfectly safe. A paternalistic Democratic machine was in control, whether it was that of Thomas Staples Martin, Bishop James Cannon, or Harry Flood Byrd. It was a government that was always basically honest and above all conservative. With a modicum of public education, but not enough to make the masses aware of the travesty upon democracy that was the government of Virginia, and, with the Negro in his place, white Virginians after 1902 had little to fear and less to crusade for.

For the Negro, the future had never been so grim since before emancipation. It was more or less true that "most of the friction . . . [which had] existed between the races since the War of Secession . . . [could] be traced directly to political agitation" [68] by both black and white. It was true, as Booker T. Washington wrote in 1901, that a mistake was made "at the beginning of our freedom of putting the emphasis on the wrong end. Politics and the holding of office were too largely emphasized, almost to the exclusion of every other interest." [69] It was also true that the Virginia Negro had voted

[65] Horn, "Growth and Development of the Democratic Party in Virginia Since 1890," Ph.D. Dissertation (Duke University, 1949), 65.

[66] McDanel, "Virginia Constitutional Convention of 1901–1902," *Johns Hopkins University Studies in Historical and Political Science*, XLVI, p. 51. For this data McDanel cites Richmond *News-Leader*, November 19, 1924.

[67] Woodward, *Origins of the New South*, 344–345, basing his computations upon figures from the *World Almanac*.

[68] Morton, *Negro in Virginia Politics*, 135.

[69] Quoted in Morton, *Negro in Virginia Politics*, 160.

in greater or lesser numbers for a third of a century, and the Commonwealth had survived and progressed. Unusual political and educational progress had been made when he voted the most fearlessly—during the Readjuster period (1879–1883). Likewise, it was true that the Negro by education and experience was far more capable of wisely exercising his suffrage rights in 1900 than he ever had been previously. He had been made the cause of fraud and election dishonesty because he had been all but deserted by his own party and then made a victim of economic and political expediency by the Democratic party. That he should now be disfranchised, along with many whites, in the name of honest elections, was the grossest sort of injustice.

Chapter 5

Social Acceptance and Unacceptance

AT THE same time that the Virginia Negro fought hopelessly for political equality, he struggled even more hopelessly for social equality. The Thirteenth Amendment to the Constitution had made his freedom a reality, but in the face of almost universal Southern opposition, the Fourteenth and Fifteenth Amendments never assured to him either equal protection under state laws or exercise of his vote without impediment. And, by the end of the century, Southern states no longer hesitated to pass laws which abridged privileges of the Negro and denied him the right to vote. The road from merely ignoring the Fourteenth and Fifteenth Amendments to openly flouting them, wound through thirty tortured years of Virginia history. Along the way, both Negroes and whites were puzzled by the inconsistencies which marked it, but the average white Virginian was far more determined that the Negro should not enjoy what was commonly termed social equality than he was determined that the Negro should not enjoy political equality. Even so, the most distinguishing factor in the complexity of social relations between the races, was that of inconsistency. From 1870–1900, there was no generally accepted code of racial morés. It is perhaps true that in a majority of the cases where a Negro presumed to demand equal treatment—in hotels, restaurants, theatres, and bars, and even on the railroads—he was more likely to meet rejection than acceptance. But uncertainty led many Negroes to keep trying for acceptance, just as it led at least some whites to accept them. Acceptance by the whites of racial intermingling on the railroads was encouraged by the propensity of the Federal courts to award damages to Negroes who charged unequal treatment.

Perhaps the best summary of the treatment of Negroes on the railroads of not only Virginia, but of the entire South, is that of this contemporary, who wrote: "On most of the railroads in the South the negroes were expected and told to take a particular car in each train, and they usually did so; but the rule did not appear to be strictly enforced." Well-dressed Negroes, claimed this observer, sometimes traveled in the first-class cars, and the more poorly-dressed whites were sometimes found in the Negro car.[1]

Until the Federal Civil Rights Act of 1866 was passed, Virginia law did not permit Negroes to ride on public street cars. Following passage of that act, a suit was brought by a group of Negroes against a Richmond street railway company to test the validity of the practiced discrimination. The result was that the right of the Negroes to ride on street cars was recognized, but two classes of cars were established—one for white women and their escorts only, and one for all persons regardless of race or sex. After Military Reconstruction began, in 1867, Negroes were allowed to ride the street cars without even this discrimination. On the railroads, however, throughout the period 1865–1870, Negroes generally were made to ride in the smoking car. This practice included Negro women and children as well as Negro men.[2]

As early as April, 1870, however, at least one Virginia railroad reportedly resorted to the use of a special or Jim Crow car for Negro passengers only, instead of assigning them indiscriminately to the smoking car. This was done by the Orange and Alexandria (now part of the Southern) Railroad. At the same time, the smoking car accommodating both races was retained.[3] To some Negroes, including Negro legislators, this was apparently an acceptable procedure. Negro opposition to discrimination by the railroads centered on the frequent practice of requiring them to ride in the smoking car, not on the use of Jim Crow cars, although there was, of course, opposition to that policy too. On January 5, 1871, a Negro member of the House of Delegates offered a resolution that a committee of three be appointed to consult with the owners of the various railroads operating in Virginia in regard to provision of special cars for the sole and exclusive use of Negro passengers. The response of the House was to reject the motion without even sending it to committee.[4] This action, however, represented not opposition to the principle

---

[1] Harrison, "Studies in the South," *Atlantic Monthly*, L (1882), 626.
[2] Taylor, "Negro in the Reconstruction of Virginia," *Journal of Negro History*, XI (1926), 294.
[3] Richmond *Daily Dispatch*, April 8, 1870.
[4] *Journal of the House of Delegates, 1870–71*, p. 79.

of segregation, but rather it represented the belief that Negroes should continue to ride in the smoking cars.

Because many Negroes objected to leaving first-class cars to ride in the Jim Crow car or the smoking car, a number of suits charging violation of the Civil Rights Act and the Fourteenth Amendment were brought in the Federal courts during the early 1870's. In January, 1871, a colored woman named Kate Cummings was awarded $1,100 damages by the U. S. Circuit Court in Richmond because she had been forcibly removed from a first-class car and made to ride in the smoking car. She had purchased a first-class ticket in New York for Lynchburg, Virginia, and had traveled first-class until she was between Washington, D. C. and Alexandria on the Orange and Alexandria line.[5] This line had begun the use of a "for colored only" car in 1870.[6] In January of 1871 the car for colored persons was either not attached to this train or was no longer being used, because one of the newspapers which reported the incident went on to advocate editorially the use of separate cars for Negroes instead of forcing them to ride in the smoking car.[7]

A number of similar cases arose the same year. J. J. Wright, Negro judge of the Supreme Court of South Carolina, purchased a first-class ticket in Charleston and rode in first-class cars in both that state and in North Carolina. But when he reached Clover Depot in Halifax county, Virginia, on the Richmond and Danville road, he was made to leave the first-class car on the personal order of Colonel Algernon S. Buford, president of the line. Wright sued the railroad for $5,000 damages but settled out of court for $1,250.[8] Also in 1871, James Sims, colored, was awarded $1,800 in damages against the Richmond, Fredericksburg, and Potomac Railroad and the Potomac Steamboat Company for being forced, in 1869, to leave the main saloon of the steamer *Keyport* even though he held a first-class ticket. Sims was a member of the Georgia legislature at the time and was traveling from Washington, D. C. to Savannah, Georgia.[9] Five years later, in 1876, a watchman at the Chesapeake and Ohio depot in Staunton was sentenced to four months imprisonment for putting

[5] Richmond *Daily Dispatch*, January 28, 1871.
[6] *Ibid.*, April 8, 1870.
[7] Harrisonburg *Old Commonwealth*, February 1, 1871.
[8] *Ibid.*, April 19, 1871.
[9] Richmond *Daily Dispatch*, May 18–19, 1871.

a Negro woman out of the passengers' waiting room.[10] In May, 1871, a Negro had been evicted from a Richmond street car set apart for the use of white persons, but no legal action had been brought.[11]

After about the middle 1870's, the frequency of such incidents greatly decreased and did not increase again. Why this is so cannot readily be determined, but there are some probable reasons, which singly or together, tend to explain the anomaly. Following the end of Military Reconstruction, white Virginians were eager to reassert their old authority over their former slaves and resented the rights which the military commanders had allowed the Negro to exercise. The Negro, on the other hand, was determined to hold on to whatever rights he had been granted [12] and to expand them if possible in face of any white opposition. By the mid-1870's, the Conservatives had generally succeeded in putting the Negro in his place and had thoroughly consolidated their hold over both politics and the Negro. As a result, the Negro not only ceased to be a major political factor,[13] but also, in despair, ceased to insist upon being granted many of his rights.

In 1873–1874, Edward King traveled through the South gathering material for his book, *The Great South*, in which he spoke of "the car where the colored people were seated" on the Gordonsville to Lynchburg, Virginia train.[14] In 1882, a Virginia Negro newspaper referred to the "Jim Crow car" in the same breath with the "negro gallery." [15] That there were Jim Crow cars, some white Virginians ashamedly admitted, as did the *Loudoun Telephone*, in 1891: "Virginia cannot afford to have the Jim Crow car stand among her other products at the [Chicago] World's Fair." [16] W. E. B. DuBois, a student at Fisk University, Nashville, Tennessee, recalled in his autobiography (without specifically stating where) separation

---

[10] Taylor, "Negro in Reconstruction of Virginia," *Journal of Negro History*, XI (1926), 295.

[11] Richmond *Daily Dispatch*, May 31, 1871.

[12] These rights, however, did not include indiscriminate seating on the railroads. Taylor, "Negro in Virginia Reconstruction," *Journal of Negro History*, XI (1926), 294.

[13] Eckenrode, "History of Virginia Since 1865," p. 94; Morton, *Negro in Virginia Politics*, 96; Martin, "Negro Disfranchisement in Virginia," *Howard University Studies in the Social Sciences*, I, p. 89.

[14] King, *Great South*, 554. This was undoubtedly the Orange and Alexandria Railroad, the line which in 1870 reportedly began using "for colored only" cars—Richmond *Daily Dispatch*, April 8, 1870.

[15] Richmond *Virginia Star*, November 11, 1882.

[16] Quoted in Sheldon, *Populism in the Old Dominion*, 35.

of the races on the railroads of the South, a practice which, he said, was just beginning.[17]

There is also evidence which indicates that racial incidents on the railroads decreased by the mid-1870's because large numbers of white Virginians, at least in some parts of the state, gradually became accustomed to Negroes riding in whatever cars and seats they chose. Thomas Wentworth Higginson, onetime abolitionist and commander of a Negro combat regiment in the Civil War, observed in 1878 that he "rode with colored people in first-class cars throughout Virginia and South Carolina, and in street cars in Richmond and Charleston." [18] In 1885, George W. Cable, critic of the South which he loved, wrote: "In Virginia they [*i.e.* the Negroes] may ride exactly as white people do and in the same cars." [19] That same year, T. McCants Stewart, a Negro newspaperman from Boston, Massachusetts, recorded how he rode in a railway car between Washington, D. C. and Petersburg, Virginia, which was so crowded that some white passengers had to sit on their luggage, while he retained his seat undisturbed by either white passengers or conductor.[20]

In the *Southern Workman*, published at The Hampton Institute, Hampton, Virginia, there appeared for many years a more or less regular column headed "Southern Sketches," and written by (Mrs.) Orra Langhorne. Born and reared in Harrisonburg, Virginia, she came of a family which, like that of her husband had owned slaves before the Civil War. At the time her column appeared, she and her husband lived in Lynchburg, but she often returned to the

---

[17] W. E. B. DuBois, *Dusk of Dawn: An Essay Toward an Autobiography of a Race Concept* (New York, 1940), 30. A Tennessee statute of 1881 provided for separate first-class accommodations for Negroes but left second-class cars unsegregated. Separation of the races on the railroads *by statute* was begun in the South in Florida, in 1887; Mississippi, 1888; Texas, 1889; Louisiana, 1890; and in Alabama, Arkansas, Kentucky, and Georgia in 1891—Woodward, *Origins of the New South*, 211 n.–212. Not till 1900 did Virginia provide by law for separation of the races on the railroads.

[18] Thomas Wentworth Higginson, "Some War Scenes Revisited," *Atlantic Monthly*, XLII (July, 1878), 7.

[19] George W. Cable, "The Silent South," *Century Magazine*, XXX (1885), 685. This article and other similar material is also available in book form—Cable, *The Silent South* (New York, 1885); Cable, *The Negro Question*, edited by Arlin Turner (New York, 1958).

[20] Cited in C. Vann Woodward, *The Strange Career of Jim Crow* (New York, 1957, revised edition), 20.

Valley by way of Charlottesville and Staunton to visit relatives still living there. Traveling by rail on these trips, she gathered material for her column. She loved Virginia but was liberal-minded in that love, and one might say that she was emancipated from the Southern tradition. Warmly human and humanitarian in her interests, she was a shrewd observer who often saw behind a gilded façade. Writing in 1890 she noted, "Colored people move about a great deal these days, and so far as those seen in my frequent trips through Virginia, they travel in cars occupied by the general public without regard to 'race, color or previous condition of servitude.' " [21] The next year she wrote: "In the various journeyings of the last year, I have always seen colored people traveling in the ladies' car, and the street cars of various cities, and have never seen any objection made by white people to their doing so." [22]

Accurately summing up the racial discrimination policies of Virginia railroads, the Richmond *State* said, in 1890: ". . . it can be said of railway travel in Virginia, on some roads at least, that he [*i.e.* the Negro] occupies whatever seats he may be pleased to take in first-class car[s]." [23]

But of all the evidence which indicates that the two races did once ride side by side on some of the state's railways, the most convincing is that offered by the state railroad commissioner himself. In his annual report for 1891, J. C. Hill, state railroad commissioner, recommended that legislation be enacted to require separation of the races in railway cars. He proposed that Virginia adopt a law similar to that of Alabama, which required provision of separate cars or compartments for each race. Noting that the question had been discussed for several years, he pointed out that the use of second-class tickets by some of the Virginia railroads had been found to be inadequate to accomplish separation of the races. Neither, he admitted, did all the railway companies in the state employ the second-class rate for separating the races.[24] Undoubtedly the matter had been discussed in some quarters for several years, as Commissioner Hill claimed, but it was a fact that none of the earlier annual reports

21 Orra Langhorne, "Southern Sketches," *Southern Workman*, August, 1890.
22 *Ibid.*, August, 1891.
23 Richmond *State*, January 7, 1890.
24 *Fifteenth Annual Report of the Railroad Commissioner of the State of Virginia* (Richmond, 1891), p. VIII.

of the railroad commissioner (dating from 1877) contained any such proposal for separation of the races.[25] Hill had been commissioner since 1887. He was still in that office when the Virginia statute of 1900 providing for separation of the races on the railroads was adopted, but only in 1891 did he ever recommend such legislation. Although it would be difficult to prove a connection, this fact should be viewed alongside the fact that the previous year (1890) had seen the inauguration of Gov. Philip W. McKinney, a man who showed little sympathy for the Negro, and who as a result was the most unpopular among Negroes of all the Virginia governors of this period.[26] Immediately after McKinney took office, Hill presented his annual report containing no recommendation for discrimination on trains. But a year later—the year of Hill's recommendation—McKinney's views and policies were much clearer. Hill's was a political office, and as shown by his long tenure in office he obviously knew how to follow the currently popular political line. Further testimony to his adroitness was his remaining in office throughout the O'Ferrall administration (1894–1898), for no Virginia governor since the Civil War was more popular with the Negroes or did more to protect them from the violence of lynch law and assure them justice before the courts, than did O'Ferrall.[27]

The majority of the evidence indicates that by the end of the nineteenth century it was customary for the races to ride together on most of the railroads of Virginia without confinement to either a Jim Crow car or the smoking car. True, there were exceptions to this practice, but as the century wore on to a close, those exceptions became fewer and fewer. By 1900, instead of referring to "the car where the Negroes rode," or "the smoking car where the Negroes were," white Virginians spoke of the "present system" when they objected to mixing of the races on trains.[28] How strongly the mass of white Virginians objected to mixing of the races on the railroads cannot readily be determined. But evidence supporting the contention that the railroad segregation statute of 1900 was passed in response to

[25] *Annual Report[s] of the Railroad Commissioner,* 1877–1890.
[26] See the Negro newspaper, Richmond *Planet,* 1890–1893, inclusive, and *Planet,* March 23, 1895; also see *Appletons' Annual Cyclopedia* (1890), 850.
[27] See the Negro newspaper, Richmond *Planet,* 1894–1897, inclusive, but especially the issue of March 23, 1895; also see *Proceedings of the Negro Protective Association.* Jackson Papers; and Morton, *Negro in Virginia Politics, 139–140.*
[28] Richmond, *Twice A Week Times,* January 12, 1900.

popular demand extending over a number of years is indeed slight
and unreliable.[29] Even the conservative newspapers fail to reflect the
alleged popular demand till late in 1899 and early in 1900. A number of racial incidents occurred on the railroads in rapid succession,
and they were blown up by those newspapers into "state-wide demand for a railroad segregation statute."

One newspaper claimed that a general demand for separate cars
arose throughout the state following an incident which took place in
December of 1899. A drunken Negro sat down by a white woman
on a Richmond-Petersburg train, and a white man forced him to
move. (At the time there were also other Negroes in the same car[30]—
further substantiation that the races did at onetime customarily
ride together in Virginia.) Shortly after, a fight occurred between
two Negroes and several white men on board a Chesapeake and
Ohio train bound from the west of the state to Richmond. The
cause was one of the Negroes' allegedly picking up a cane belonging
to a white man near whom he was sitting.[31] Such incidents had undoubtedly occurred before, creating little if any more disturbance
than would have been caused by a drunken white man sitting by a
white woman or by a white man allegedly stealing another's cane.
Weight was added to the case for segregation, however, in an alleged incident involving Virginia Governor J. Hoge Tyler. While
on his way by train to Atlanta, Georgia, in late 1899, Tyler reportedly awoke in the morning in his sleeping compartment to find
"a negro opposite him, above him, and in front of him." [32] Within
three months after this incident, the Virginia legislature enacted the
law of 1900 *requiring* railroads operating in the state to furnish separate cars or coaches for the white and Negro races. In 1906, after

---

[29] This is the contention of Morton, *Negro in Virginia Politics*, 141. As evidence
Morton cites the Governor's Message to the General Assembly, 1891–1892. The
governor at that time was Philip W. McKinney, who was not noted for friend-
liness toward the Negro, and who was in consequence unpopular with the Negro
—Richmond *Planet*, 1890–1893, inclusive and *Appletons' Annual Cyclopedia*
(1890), 850. It was also during McKinney's administration in which there was
made the only recommendation by the State Railroad Commisioner that the races
be separated on the railroads—*Report of the Railroad Commissioner*, 1891, p.
VIII. The year of this recommendation corresponds with that of the governor's
message cited by Morton.
[30] Richmond *Twice A Week Times*, January 12, 1900.
[31] *Ibid.*, January 9, 1900.
[32] Quoted in Writers' Program of the WPA, *Negro in Virginia*, 241. Source of
the quotation not stated.

experimenting with a law *authorizing* and *empowering* companies operating street cars to separate the races, a law was enacted *requiring* separation of the races on the street cars.[33] The famous *Plessy vs. Fergusson* Supreme Court decision of 1896 gave further impetus to the case for segregation. In this celebrated case, the court upheld the legality of an 1890 Louisiana statute which required provision of "separate but equal" accommodations for the two races on the railroads of the state. Soon that principle was to lend the legal basis to the myriad, Southern Jim Crow laws. It is significant that Virginia waited for four years after this decision before enacting her separate railroad accommodations statute, and that the decision itself seemed to prompt no popular demand for racial separation.

Thus in thirty years the Negro had moved from the railway smoking car and a few Jim Crow cars to acceptance in first-class accommodations on most Virginia railroads, and then back to the Jim Crow car in every case. His was an odyssey of sorrow, of hope, and finally despair, since much that he had gained since 1865, including the suffrage and the recognized right to ride the trains and street cars as an equal, was swept away from him by a rash of legislation based upon white supremacy.

Much less successful than the Negro's search for equality of treatment on the state's railroads was his search for equal preferment in restaurants, hotels, bars, and theatres. Only in isolated cases did he meet with acceptance. Insistence upon these rights in nearly all instances met with cold rejection or physical eviction. However, it must be recognized that, unlike the situation of the railroads, there were very few public hostels or places of amusement from which Negroes sought service. In those years, anyone who journeyed more than a few miles from home almost always traveled by train, including poor whites and Negroes. But the Negroes, poor, ignorant, and often unaware of such luxuries, generally did not seek admittance to public establishments providing personal services or amusements. It was easy to rebuff the few who did. Besides, the majority of those seeking these things were travelers or visitors from outside the state, who were not prone to make an issue of discrimination they met only in passing. An out-of-state Negro visitor's being refused service in a Virginia restaurant was quite a different

<hr />
[33] *Acts of the General Assembly of the State of Virginia, 1899–1900,* pp. 236–237; *Code of Virginia* (1904), 681; *Code of Virginia* (1919), I, p. 1595.

matter from that same visitor's buying a first-class railroad ticket in New York, for instance, only to be refused first-class accommodations when the train reached Virginia.

Throughout this period, public inns and hotels did not admit Negroes unless they catered solely to a Negro clientele.[34] In July, 1874, James Hayne Rainey, Negro congressman from South Carolina, entered a hotel dining room in Suffolk and was promptly thrown out forcibly.[35] Rare indeed were such incidents as that related in 1885 by T. McCants Stewart, the Northern Negro newspaperman. Leaving a train on which he had ridden without any evidence of discrimination, Stewart entered a railroad station dining room south of Petersburg, "bold as a lion," and sat down at a table with white people. He was politely served while the white diners appeared not to notice him.[36] It should be remembered that the station dining room which Stewart entered was on a railroad which apparently did not resort to racial discrimination on its trains. The dining room probably belonged to the railroad or else catered to the railroad's passengers. Hence this incident becomes much less indicative of any policy of non-discrimination followed by Virginia restaurants. It does, however, indicate that at least one of the railroads which gave Negroes equal treatment on their trains gave them the same treatment in station dining rooms.

In an attempt to protect the Negro from discrimination on public conveyances, in restaurants, hotels, theatres, and other places of amusement, Congress passed the Supplementary Civil Rights Act of 1875. Forbidding discrimination because of "race, color or previous condition of servitude," the new law was a mere irritant to the South, which proceeded to violate it with impunity. Nevertheless, most Southerners were relieved when, in 1883, the Supreme Court declared it unconstitutional. An Arkansas newspaper commented: "Society is a law unto itself which in matters social in nature overrides the statutes. Against its decrees the written law is powerless."[37] As far as the Civil Rights Act was concerned, that

---

[34] Taylor, "Negro in the Reconstruction of Virginia," *Journal of Negro History,* XI (1926), 296.

[35] Samuel Denny Smith, *The Negro in Congress, 1870–1901* (Chapel Hill, N. C., 1940), 47.

[36] Cited in Woodward, *Strange Career of Jim Crow,* 20.

[37] Quoted in John Hope Franklin, "History of Racial Segregation in the United States," *Annals of the American Academy of Political and Social Science,* CCCIV (March, 1956), 5.

statement was correct, because the Supreme Court decision held, in effect, that Congress had no power to legislate in the area of social rights for the Negro.[38] This court decision was of little practical import, because as noted above, the South had violated the Civil Rights Act with impunity and as *The Nation* pointed out at the time of the law's passage, few Negroes sought to use the hotels and other public places anyway.[39] The New York *Tribune* observed that the law had done nothing except "irritate public feeling and keep alive antagonism between the races," because few Negroes could afford to bring suit in court even if done an injustice. Besides, said the *Tribune*, Negroes were not disposed to force themselves into hotels and the better theatre seats.[40]

As the *Tribune* claimed, Negroes generally did not insist upon sitting in the better theatre seats. Instead, they usually went without question to the gallery or other portion set aside for them. J. B. Harrison noted how Negroes were ushered to a gallery at public and theatrical functions in Norfolk and Richmond. If they insisted, however, they were permitted to sit in the main auditorium unless it was so crowded that they could not sit by themselves in the back or to one side, as they voluntarily did. Then they were directed, but apparently not forced, to go to the gallery; Harrison was told that if they insisted upon sitting among the whites, all the whites near them would have moved.[41] A week-long disturbance was created in Richmond in 1886 when a Negro member of the New York delegation to the Knights of Labor annual convention entered a theatre with white friends and sat down in the midst of the whites. Several white people left the theatre rather than remain seated near him.[42] A similar incident in Richmond in 1875 concerned two very light-skinned mulattoes attending the play *Davy Crockett*. When on the point of being forced to retire to the colored section, one of them left the theatre. When some of the men congregated in a saloon across the street after the play, a fight ensued between a John Snellings and a young man described as being "well known" in Richmond business circles, because the latter admitted that he had

[38] L. E. Murphy, "The Civil Rights Law of 1875," *Journal of Negro History* XII (April, 1927), 126.
[39] Cited in *Ibid.*, 124.
[40] Cited in *Ibid.*, 125.
[41] Harrison, "Studies in the South," *Atlantic Monthly*, L (1882), 626.
[42] Richmond *Daily Dispatch*, October 5, 7, 8, 9, 10, 13, 1886.

bought the ticket for one of the Negroes. The *Dispatch* did not name the "well known" businessman.[43] In Bedford (then known as Bedford City) in 1891, Sandy Hadue, colored, presented reserved tickets for himself and a colored companion at the local opera house, but was directed to the section set aside for Negroes, because Negroes had "never before occupied those [*i.e.* the reserved] seats."[44] The only public entertainments which the Negro was sure of meeting no racial discrimination were circuses or other carnival-like events usually found in the smaller towns.[45]

Discrimination extended even to the use of public buildings for all-Negro official functions. A request to use the Harrisonburg town hall for graduation exercises in 1884 for the local colored school was firmly refused. Many white people attended the same commencement when held at the Negro school,[46] however, and in this same Valley town, both white and black were kept in one almshouse.[47] Whether they dined and lived together is not clear.

Lewis H. Blair, Richmond business man and outspoken liberal, accurately summed up the situation in his forthright book:

> In the capital of our great country, the respectable negro, though not welcomed, is admitted to the best hotels, to the best seats in theatres . . . and in presidential receptions he meets with no humiliating discriminations; yet when we come south as far as Richmond . . . we seem to be in a different country, we seem to be transplanted from a world of equality where worth makes the man to a land of caste where birth makes him. In Richmond a riot is threatened when it is thought that a negro member of a Brooklyn white lodge intends occupying in company with his white brother, a first-class seat in the theatre. The hotels, except under extraordinary pressure [*sic*] drive negroes from their doors; . . . and if a negro with his wife . . . were to attend the governor's public reception, they would in a few minutes be the only guests, or they would be frozen, if not driven out.[48]

---

[43] *Ibid.*, March 9, 1875.
[44] Richmond *Weekly Times*, December 31, 1891.
[45] Taylor, "Negro in the Reconstruction of Virginia," *Journal of Negro History*, XI (1926), 296.
[46] Hampton, *Southern Workman*, September, 1884.
[47] *Ibid.*, October, 1886.
[48] Blair, *Prosperity of the South Dependent Upon the Elevation of the Negro*, 60–61. Blair was important enough for the conservative Lyon G. Tyler (editor) to list in the *Encyclopedia of Virginia Biography* (New York, 1915), III, p. 185, but it is no wonder that he was spoken of as having views which would "never achieve popularity south of the Potomac."

It is significant, however, that Blair claimed Richmond hotels drove Negroes from their doors, "except under extraordinary pressure." This statement implies that they *were* accepted in some instances. No other evidence in support of this has been found, but this does not mean that some Negroes were not admitted to the hotels, for the newspapers and the other contemporary records of that day were prone to publicize Negro rejection, not acceptance. Still, as Blair intimated, such instances were rare.

It was an exceptional instance when white and black met socially on the Negro's own ground, such as the private Hampton Institute. Here, at the African Methodist annual conference of 1879, General Samuel C. Armstrong, principal of the (then) Hampton Normal School, told delegates that in May, 1878, former slave-holders had dined with colored men and women at the Hampton examinations of that year.[49]

Rarer still, were instances where the white man met the black man privately and socially. In 1884, the Rockingham county superintendent of schools, a Readjuster appointee, entertained at dinner in his home a Negro minister, the brother of one of his teachers. For this, the press and the populace heaped abuse upon him.[50] Governor Charles T. O'Ferrall (1894–1898) as staunch a friend as the Negro had in official position between 1865 and 1900, nevertheless drew the line on social relations with him. While he might do all he could to assure justice and prevent lynch violence,[51] the governor was not prepared to meet the Negro socially. In 1895, O'Ferrall received a visiting state delegation from Massachusetts unaware that there was to be a Negro in the group. To Massachusetts State Senator Thomas W. Darling, who had headed the delegation, he later wrote:

> The time has not come when I would knowingly invite a committee of any kind in which there was a colored man to dine or lunch at my private house or the Gubernatorial Mansion. . . . candor requires me to say that if it had been intimated to me that a colored man was in your party my attentions would have been much more formal than they were and you would have been received at my Executive Office

---

[49] Rev. Israel L. Butt, *History of African Methodism in Virginia: or Four Decades in the Old Dominion* (Hampton, Va., 1908), n.p.

[50] Hampton *Southern Workman*, September, 1884.

[51] Richmond *Planet*, March 23, 1895; *Proceedings of the Negro Protective Association.* Jackson Papers; Morton, *Negro in Virginia Politics*, 139–140.

and not at the Mansion; for I draw the line on the Negro at the social circle or anywhere else that suggests even a semblance of social equality.[52]

It was plain to the Negroes that socially they were unwanted, and as a consequence most of them simply did not insist upon equal social privileges even when they were in a position to do so. The following particular incident is of little significance in itself, but it does indicate how *many* Negroes meekly accepted the position of an inferior status. In Wise county of far-Southwest Virginia, there lived a former slave named Dan Richmond. His home was on Black Mountain near present-day Big Stone Gap. Places to stop overnight in that area were far apart, and on at least one occasion a white man requested lodging for the night. Richmond received him hospitably and gave him a clean bed in a room by himself. He was served a "delicious and substantial" meal at a separate table before Richmond and his family ate. All offer of payment was refused.[53]

The observations of contemporaries from abroad all bore out this general picture, although their observations were usually drawn from the broader American scene. The distinguished English historian Edward A. Freeman observed: "I need hardly say that I never met a negro at any American gentleman's table." [54] The French *Comte* Alessandro Zannini was so struck by the practice of segregation in the United States in the early 1880's that he wrote (in *De L'Atlantique An Mississippi*, Paris, 1884, p. 59):

. . . there is not a white man in America who would stoop so low as to share his table with a Negro. A black man may be a millionaire but he will never be received in a suitable hotel. At the theater he is often in a separate place. White servants refuse him their service; and strange as it may seem, Negroes themselves do not voluntarily serve their fellowmen.[55]

[52] Charles T. O'Ferrall to Senator Francis [actually Thomas] W. Darling, March 21, 189[5]. O'Ferrall Executive Papers, box no. 372 (Virginia State Library, Richmond, Virginia).
[53] Charles A. Johnson, *A Narrative History of Wise County, Virginia* (Kingsport, Tenn., 1938), 293–295.
[54] Edward A. Freeman, *Some Impressions of the United States* (New York, 1883), 148.
[55] Translated by and quoted in Evans James Bonaparte, "The Negro in the Writings of French and British Travelers to the United States, 1877–1900," Unpublished M. A. Thesis (Howard University, 1948), 37.

James Lord Bryce, astute British critic of American institutions, found almost no social mixing of the races even in the North. And unlike Virginia's Lewis H. Blair,[56] he did not exclude Washington, D. C.

> Except on the Pacific coast, a negro man never sits down to dinner with a white man in a railway refreshment room. You never encounter him at a private party. He is not received in a hotel of the better sort, no matter how rich he may be. He will probably be refused a glass of soda water at a drug store. He is not shaved in a place frequented by white men, not even by a barber of his own color. He worships in a church of his own. No white woman would dream of receiving his addresses. Nor does it make any difference that he is three parts or seven parts white, if the stain of colour can still be discerned. Kindly condescension is the best he can look for, accompanied by equality of access to a business or profession. Social equality is utterly out of reach.[57]

Another English visitor, William Saunders, found in Virginia that white and black no longer met together in Good Templar Lodges, "as they formerly did" [58] (presumably during Military Reconstruction). Saunders continued:

> I never saw white and coloured men in friendly conversation, and so great is the separation that not in a single instance did I find white and colored children playing together. As fellow workmen, and as master and servant, the two races get on well, but socially there seems to be an impassable barrier between them.[59]

An anonymous English visitor wrote:

> . . . the color line in social matters is not likely ever to be broken through. A gradually diminishing minority [sic] is not likely to wrest a privilege from a ruling and increasing majority, the concession of which that same majority now looks on as a calamity worse than death itself.[60]

---

[56] Blair, *Prosperity of the South Dependent Upon the Elevation of the Negro*, 60–61.

[57] James Bryce, *The American Commonwealth* (New York and London, 1895, third edition), II, pp. 503–504.

[58] William Saunders, *Through the Light Continent: or the United States in 1877–8* (London, Paris, and New York, 1879), 78.

[59] *Ibid.*, 78–79.

[60] Anonymous, "A Social Study of Our Oldest Colony," *Littell's Living Age*, CLXI (1884), 370.

The Virginia scholar, Philip Alexander Bruce, observed that,

. . . intercourse between the children of the two races [such as was common and accepted in slavery days] is rarely observed now, because the white people are, as a rule, strict in forbidding theirs to turn to such society for diversion. They are induced to do this, primarily, by antipathy of race that makes them careful to preserve the barriers between the negroes and themselves . . . which, they believe, can only be done by keeping the two races as far apart socially as possible.[61]

No wonder that W. E. B. DuBois declared in a social study of Negro life in Farmville, in 1897, that the Negroes there resorted to "group life," having their own churches, organizations, and social life, and mixed with the whites only in the economic area! [62]

When he was relegated to the Jim Crow car by statute in 1900 and disfranchised by the new constitution in 1902, the Virginia Negro lost most of what he had gained since 1865 except his legal freedom and the right to a minimum of public education. Thus, the beginning of the new century marked the birth of a new era in race relations which would see the perfection of the code of racial discrimination and segregation. But in the world of social acceptance at hotels, inns, restaurants, bars, theatres, and other places of amusement, and in the homes and other private circles of the white man, the Virginia Negro had gained nothing which he could lose; for in those areas, by 1900, he stood in essentially the same place and in the same relation to the white man in which he had stood in 1865.

---

[61] Philip Alexander Bruce, *The Plantation Negro as a Freeman* (New York and London, 1889), 52.

[62] W. E. B. DuBois, "The Negroes of Farmville, Virginia: A Social Study," *Bulletin of the Department of Labor, III* (1898), 34.

Chapter 6

White Attitudes toward the Negro

WHITE attitudes toward the new freedom of the Negro were definite and clear. A majority of the whites who left records resented the Negro's new status. Some were bitter and uncompromising in their resentment, while others resignedly tolerated what they regarded as the inevitable. Still others held out hope and toleration for the Negro in the early years following the war, only to lose it in anger and frustration by about 1890. This was due primarily to the constant political turbulence created by the temptation of the Negro to seek his whole salvation in politics, and the temptation of both major parties to use the Negro for their own selfish ends.

Prejudice toward him socially was always more uncompromising, although that too, in some areas, seemed to harden after 1890. The overwhelming majority of white Virginians, whatever their own social and economic status, were determined that those who had been slaves and the descendants of slaves, should not associate equally with them as free men.

The chief source for ascertaining white Virginians' attitudes toward the Negro is the newspapers of the state. The mass of white Virginians, like the mass of Negro Virginians, left no written records. These newspapers were, however, guilty of over-reporting mere rumors and of paying too little attention to ascertaining the real facts. Likewise, they were given to emotional and occasionally vituperative editorials. All of them did a better job of molding public opinion than accurately reporting the news. With few exceptions,[1] most of the papers were also basically conservative, Democratic, and naturally given to supporting the conservative wing of the Democrats. When the newspapers reported on the race situation all these

---

[1] Notable among them being, the Richmond *Whig*, Abingdon *Virginian*, and the Luray *Page Courier*, all Readjuster papers. There were a few others too, mostly small town or county papers. And some readers might insist upon adding at least one of the larger city papers, for example the Richmond *Times*, but that paper was instrumental in reporting the state-wide demand for racial segregation on the trains in 1900—a demand whose existence one might charitably call highly dubious.

criticisms were compounded, for it was in that area that the newspapers of the late nineteenth century were at their worst. A reporter for the London *Times* observed that, to be informed on the race situation in America, one had to read the county and other small newspapers, not those of the big cities.[2] His observation was especially apt in the case of Virginia, but there as elsewhere, one had to also be very selective and judicious in reading even the small local papers. General Samuel C. Armstrong, principal of Hampton Institute, said in 1879 that the progress in Southern sentiment toward the Negro which had taken place in the previous decade was apparent only if one looked "behind the front presented by politicians and periodicals."[3]

Poor as they are, state newspapers must still be cited as the most complete, if not the best, record available. A better record, but one not nearly so complete, is to be found in the publications of non-American visitors. Often trained writers and scholars who could look at the American scene with detachment, they actually talked to the average Virginian for whom the newspapers claimed to speak.

We know little about what the typical, average, white Virginian thought. The following story, while not definitive, is indicative. The Richmond *Dispatch* was always in the forefront of those who doubted not only the Negro's ethical and intellectual right to hold office, but also even his ability to cast an intelligent vote. In 1872, the *Dispatch* editorially opposed any party's bidding for the Negro vote and maintained that there was *no* place in politics for the Negro. In the words of the *Dispatch*, "To bid for the negro [vote] but increases his sense of self importance. . . ."[4] And on the Negro in office, the *Dispatch* earlier said: "The plain and just inference . . . from the fact that negroes are not in office, is that they are not fit for responsible positions. . . . There is, indeed, not one in twenty who are forced upon the public councils that has the slightest capability for the position he occupies. . . ."[5] To this charge, the Negro historian Luther P. Jackson replied three-quarters of a century later that

[2] W. Laird Clowes, *Black America: A Study of the Ex-Slave and his Late Master* (London, 1891), 127–128.
[3] Harriet Beecher Stowe, "The Education of Freedmen," part 2, *North American Review*, CXXIX (July, 1879), 92.
[4] Richmond *Daily Dispatch*, May 2, 1872.
[5] *Ibid.*, February 4, 1871.

Negro officeholders in Virginia "met the standards for officeholding according to the standards of their day." [6] Of their education, he said that it "corresponded very closely to the amount obtained by officeholders generally in the United States in the nineteenth century." [7] But it was not the matter of education and training which caused the *Dispatch* to oppose Negro officeholders. Twenty years later it wrote of Oberlin-educated John Mercer Langston, "While Langston is one of the best educated men of his race, he is still a negro, with all of a negro's conceit, pomposity, credulity, and stupidity." [8] It was the race, not the individual man, who was condemned.

The *Dispatch* was not alone. Referring to Petersburg in 1874, where the Negroes outnumbered the whites eleven to nine, a writer in *The Nation* observed that, "Nine years of emancipation have removed not one solitary whit of the Southern conviction of the negro's worthlessness as a legislator." [9] Campbell was told by one of the white natives of the same city that whatever seats the Negroes had won in the legislature they won by "hard voting"; and that the whites were not readily willing to concede a minority of seats to them. [10]

Scholarly studies made in recent years have generally borne out the above picture of white attitudes toward Negro suffrage and Negro officeholders. Luther P. Jackson claimed that while good feeling existed between individuals of the separate races, the white people as a whole were hostile to Negro officeholders in particular and to Negro suffrage in general. This hostility, he correctly maintained, increased with the years. And the most intelligent and capable Negro was as objectionable as the most incapable and illiterate one. [11] H. J. Eckenrode claimed that while the white people of Virginia were willing to *tolerate* Negro suffrage, at least during the Readjuster years (1879–1883), they would not accept rule by him in any degree. [12]

This, however, does not represent the whole story, because white Virginians did on occasion vote for a Negro in preference to a white carpetbagger or scalawag. [13] In 1876, Louisa county had a colored

---

[6] Jackson, *Negro Office-Holders in Virginia*, 55.
[7] *Ibid.*, 48.
[8] Richmond *Daily Dispatch*, September 26, 1890.
[9] *The Nation*, XVIII (March 26, 1874), 196–197.
[10] Campbell, *White and Black*, 282.
[11] Jackson, *Negro Office-Holders in Virginia*, 84.
[12] Eckenrode, "History of Virginia Since 1865," p. 199.
[13] Jackson, *Negro Office-Holders in Virginia*, 84.

superintendent of the poor who was "pronounced the best superintendent the county has had in many years."[14] Especially on the local scene relations were often better than they appeared on a statewide basis. Upon the death of Josiah Crump, a colored member of the Richmond board of aldermen in 1890, his fellow members adopted a resolution praising his "courteous and kindly bearing" and recognizing faithful and conscientious discharge of duties while being "ever watchful of the interests of the city."[15]

Campbell was told by General Armstrong of Hampton Institute that while the whites would not submit to being ruled by the blacks, they were not against letting the latter have a minority representation in the legislature.[16] The *Southern Workman* claimed that by 1889 many white Virginians had come to accept the fact that nearly all the Negroes voted Republican while the whites voted Democratic. The Negroes, it was said, usually accepted the practice also.[17] But few white Virginians could accept any great measure of Negro political advancement with the equanimity of philosophy professor Noah K. Davis, of the University of Virginia. Writing in the *Forum*, Davis said:

What shall we care whether the laws, so they be laws, be made by white or black. We want in Congress men of capacity, honesty, strength. Color is non-essential. . . . The time may come when a negro shall be our Secretary of State; and who will be foolish enough to object? With a sublime faith in the vigor of Anglo-Saxon blood, we do not apprehend the dominance of any other race, but hopefully look forward to the day when the best men, regardless of their origin, shall be our public servants.[18]

While it was distasteful to perhaps a majority of white Virginians to have Negroes participate in lawmaking, enforcement of the laws by Negro policemen seems to have been even more objectionable. In 1872, the *Dispatch* observed darkly with rustic suspicion,

. . . to fill our streets with negro policemen would be to ruin the business of Richmond.
. . . we should rather see negroes in many other places than to see

[14] Staunton *Spectator*, July 25, 1876.
[15] Jackson, *Negro Office-Holders in Virginia*, 84.
[16] Campbell, *White and Black*, 277.
[17] Hampton *Southern Workman*, February, 1890.
[18] Noah K. Davis, "The Negro in the South," *Forum*, I (April, 1886), 134–135.

them policemen, because policemen have charge of much property and many other things.[19]

In 1873, that same paper editorially declared: "We object to negro policemen and negro officials of every sort, because we are confident that the whites will not peacefully submit to arrest and detention and trial at their hands. . . ."[20] Contending that white Virginians felt an especial antipathy toward Negro policemen, Eckenrode cites an instance in Surry county, in 1885. When a Negro was elected constable and went to post his bond of $2,000, it was suddenly raised to $2,500, according to the *Whig*.[21] The Valley and the West were apparently not so prejudiced, at least until the twentieth century. In 1874–1875, Harrisonburg had a colored policeman, Joseph T. Williams, who had been born free but who had been a servant with the Confederate Army.[22]

As has been shown, the greatest antipathy toward the Negro lay in the social area. To the black man, social equality usually meant only the right to equal enjoyment of the privileges afforded by such public establishments as hotels, theatres, restaurants, and railroads without discrimination because of race. But to the white man it meant vastly more and called up visions of intermarriage and "mongrelization" of the races. The *Dispatch* emphatically declared in 1871: "It is idle for the negro to suppose that there is to be any social equality between the black and the white races here."[23] The press proposed that if necessary, hotels and inns surrender their licenses and become private boarding houses to maintain separation of the races socially in the face of civil rights legislation.[24] With an air of lordly gentility the *Dispatch* aptly summed up the philosophy of the most respectable white Conservatives toward the Negro:

> We [referring to the Conservative party] do not "clamour" against the negro, but only against his elevation to the social plane occupied by white men. We want no negro officers and no mixed schools. We are willing to be taxed for the education of his children, and to let him

[19] Richmond *Daily Dispatch*, May 2, 1872.
[20] *Ibid.*, April 28, 1873.
[21] Eckenrode, "History of Virginia Since 1865," pp. 193–194.
[22] John W. Wayland, *A History of Rockingham County* (Dayton, Virginia, 1912), 240–241.
[23] Richmond *Daily Dispatch*, January 11, 1871.
[24] Taylor, "Negro in the Reconstruction of Virginia," *Journal of Negro History*, XI (1926), 296.

vote in peace; but we do not want to meet him in our box at the theatre, by our side at the hotel table, and in our room in an inn, our pew at church, or our seat on a railroad car. We would never so much as hurt his feelings if we could help it, much less would we injure him. All we ask of him is to keep his place. He can ride in the chariot of Government, but the white man must drive.[25]

Two years later, in 1875, referring to the proposed civil rights bill, the *Dispatch* said:

Social comingling, or fraternization of the white and black races, is an impossibility. All the laws that Congress can pass, backed by all the powers of the Government . . . cannot enforce it.[26]

This was the organ of Conservatism speaking and its views are not surprising. But even the *Whig*, voice of Mahone and the Readjusters, sought to free the party of the charge of advocating social equality by declaring during the heated campaign of 1883:

As to men's private or social relations, that is a matter in nowise concerned in the question of political equality. All citizens, whether white or otherwise, have the equal right, under the laws of the United States and of this State, to vote and to be voted for, and to be appointed to any political office in the Commonwealth. But, when it comes to a question of sociology, men will hold their own prejudices without question, and decide such questions for themselves, according to the spirit and taste of the age and community in which they live.

. . . our party . . . encourages each race to develop its own sociology separately and apart from unlawful contamination with each other,[27] but under a government which recognizes and protects the civil rights of all equally.[28]

This, of course, was the voice of Southern moderates and not of political and social radicals which the Conservatives claimed the Readjusters to be.

With individuals, prejudice went deep. While some would admit that the Negro might by diligence lift himself to the highest positions and that most of the race might make great social and economic

---

[25] Richmond *Daily Dispatch*, August 1, 1873.
[26] *Ibid.*, March 10, 1875.
[27] This was in obvious reference to a Virginia law of 1873 forbidding intermarriage. Virginia was among the first Southern states to pass such a law— Tennessee in 1870 and North Carolina and Virginia in 1873. (Lewinson, *Race, Class, and Party*, 61.)
[28] Richmond *Weekly Whig*, September 21, 1883.

advancements, those same white individuals slammed the door on social equality. Said the enlightened and realistic Noah K. Davis:

> [The Negro] will acquire property, and with it social independence. We shall see, or our children shall see, white servants and laborers under negro employers. Resistance would be vain, and regret senseless. Brains, not color, must settle rank.
>
> But what about social intercourse? That is another thing. There is a race instinct, given by the Creator, which must forever check fusion. A negro may be my superior in wealth, intelligence and piety, but he may not sit in my social circle, or at my table, or be entertained as a guest in my home. . . . We will be true to our blood. So, too, let the negro be.[29]

While white and black rubbed shoulders in the work-a-day world, a chasm remained between them socially.

> Individuals representing both [races] are constantly thrown with each other, it is true; negroes and white men meet as employers and employees, or as common laborers; but their association stops there, and it is of a formal character as far as it goes. The two distinct societies do not join, when they come together at all, in such a way as to result in a complete blending, however brief, of their separate systems.[30]

With perception born of long years among both white and black Virginians and with a trained and practiced pen to express it, Philip A. Bruce captured the subtleties of the strange, contradictory, and kindly, yet insidious relationship which bound white and black Southerners together while it kept them poles apart at the same time.

> That the white people entertain a deep-seated social antipathy to the negro is manifest to the most careless observer; but whether this is due to the contempt and disdain which were bred in them by his former degraded condition, when his social inferiority was legalized; or whether it is to be laid at the door of his intellectual ignorance, personal uncleanliness, and moral infirmities, now that he is free; or whether it should be attributed after all to a narrow and unthinking prejudice that originates in a mere difference of color, is open to discussion. The strong probability is that this state of feeling is the result of all these powerful influences combined; but to whatever it should be ascribed, it has had a very vigorous and far-reaching effect in con-

---

[29] Davis, "The Negro in the South," *Forum*, I (April, 1886), 133–134.
[30] Bruce, *Plantation Negro as a Freeman*, 48.

firming an independent tendency of the negro to live apart to himself. No one is more conscious than he of this underlying sentiment in the hearts of the white people; he knows very well that beneath the surface of their kindness to him, even when it takes the form of the most open and sincere affection, there lurks an active and resolute sensitiveness that would rise in alarm the instant he sought, unwittingly or intentionally, to cross the social dead-line. However genial, therefore, or however friendly their demeanor to him, he is fully aware that one forward act or venturous word on his part would, at once, enkindle that emotion of repugnance which is always smouldering in their breasts, and which only requires the application of the proper match to set it aflame. The social attitude of the white people towards him is remarkable. Their conduct, capricious, irregular, and inconsistent as it seems, is yet governed by an unwritten law, that is never changed and never relaxed. In the midst of the most familiar intercourse, apparently, there is an unconscious mental reservation, an instinctive assumption of superiority by them, that gives the association a peculiar character, which the negro, heedless and impulsive as he is, appreciates by intuition. Even now, when the white people are so much more guarded in their demeanor than they were in the era of slavery, they often bear themselves towards him in a way that would be an admission of social equality, but for this subtle difference of spirit. As soon, however, as the bare idea of such equality is suggested to their minds by his manner of accepting such advances, they shrink back with unconcealed disgust and resentment, or show their indignation in a still more unmistakable way. The very fear of being misunderstood causes them to be much more circumspect in their social relations with him than they would otherwise be. All those social condescensions on their part that did so much to alleviate the hardships of slavery are, in consequence, neglected almost entirely in their present association with his race.[31]

Foreign observers vouched for the presence of this strange relationship. At the end of the century, French-Canadian Edmond Nevers, noted that, "Prejudice of English speaking people against Negroes seems invincible." He accounted for this obstinancy in the South by asserting that white Southerners had "created between themselves and their ex-slaves barriers of social disfranchisement." Meanwhile "measures of exclusion and ostracism . . . acquired the force of law and had become a group of unwritten statutes that no one dared

---

[31] *Ibid.*, 44–46.

break." [32] Other observers noted no improvement in Negro-white social relationships. [33]

The Richmond *Times*, in 1900, held that, "The black man must build his own society, for race prejudice, if nothing else, is sufficient to keep him from entering into the inner circle of the white man." [34]

In an essay generally tolerant of Negro rights, the agricultural historian Lewis Cecil Gray declared with finality early in the twentieth century that, "The question of social equality should be eliminated for the present. It is an absolute impossibility in the Southern States, whatever its ultimate desirability." [35]

That white and black should freely marry was the ultimate nightmare of the white Southerner fearing social equality. The frequency of such unions was sufficient to lead the state in 1873 to adopt a law punishing the white party. [36] From the Richmond *Enquirer* alone, Taylor cites over two-dozen such unions between 1865 and 1870. [37] Following the end of Military Reconstruction, such relationships continued to take place throughout the state—in Roanoke, Smyth, Amelia, Augusta, Buckingham, Cumberland, Charles City, Henrico, Wythe, and Prince Edward counties, [38] and probably in others as well. In Augusta county there were at least five cases of mixed marriages, and in Buckingham there were at least four. [39] These marriages were usually broken up and the parties harried from the community or even from the state. In Wythe county, a white woman who had been living with a Negro man was tarred and feathered before she was run out of the community. [40] But in at least one instance, a successful Negro farmer, horse trader, politician, and preacher, R. T. Coleman of Cumberland county, was left unmolested with each

---

[32] Translated by and quoted in Bonaparte, "Negro in the Writings of French and British Travelers to the U. S.," M. A. Thesis (Howard University, 1948), 124.

[33] George Nestler Tricoche, *La Question Des Noirs Aux Etats-Unis* (Paris, 1894), 15–16.

[34] Richmond *Twice A Week Times*, January 16, 1900.

[35] Lewis Cecil Gray, *Southern Agriculture, Plantation System, and the Negro Problem* (Philadelphia, Pa., (?) n.d.), 99.

[36] *Virginia Code* (1873), 1208.

[37] Taylor, "Negro in the Reconstruction of Virginia," *Journal of Negro History*, XI (1926), 299–301.

[38] *Ibid.*, 301–303; Richmond *Daily Dispatch*, January 28, 1870 and June 14, 1871. For his source, Taylor cites the Richmond papers, *Daily Dispatch*, *Enquirer*, and *Whig*.

[39] *Ibid.*, 303–304.

[40] Richmond *Daily Dispatch*, June 14, 1871.

of three white wives, all of whom he outlived. When he married the
third time he got around the Virginia statute of 1873 by maintaining
his white wife in a separate house next to his own.[41]

The statute of 1873 provided for only a maximum punishment of
one year in prison and a fine of one-hundred dollars *against the white
party.*[42] Nevertheless, black and white continued to intermarry after
that date, sometimes going out of the state to do so and then returning.[43] To halt this, the legislature, declaring mixed marriages as
"offenses against morality and decency," provided in 1878 for a
two-to-five-year prison sentence for mixed couples who left the state
to marry and then returned. Still they apparently continued to
marry, because in the next year, 1879, the legislature declared
mixed marriages as null and void and defined a Negro as anyone
with one-fourth Negro ancestry. Finally, in the twentieth century, in
an increasing frenzy of white supremacy, the legislature twice more
legally defined a Negro. In 1910, everyone who had one-sixteenth
Negro ancestry was declared to be legally a Negro. In 1930, the ratio
was decreased to "any" Negro ancestry.[44] Now without doubt, many
Anglo-Saxons would go through life not knowing that they were in
reality Negroes—by law!

The French visitor Henri Gaullieur felt that no nation or empire in
history had drawn so sharp a demarcation on the question of marriage as had Virginia by 1890. "The spirit of caste is so strong in this
regard that one searches in vain in the history of Rome or a lesser age
for a sharper demarcation between two human classes." [45]

Following emancipation, there increasingly developed about the
illicit relations between white men and black women an air of opprobrium formerly unknown. While the pre-war South was not
proud of such relations, it was nevertheless accepted as inevitable
that even some of the best white men would take advantage of their
colored female slaves. No social equality was apparently inferred,
however. Freedom changed all this. Such practices might now be
construed as at least a temporary admission of social equality. Now

[41] Taylor, "Negro in the Reconstruction of Virginia," *Journal of Negro History*
XI (1926), 304.
[42] *Virginia Code* (1873), 1208.
[43] Taylor, "Negro in the Reconstruction of Virginia," *Journal of Negro History,*
XI (1926), 303.
[44] Writers Program of the WPA, *Negro in Virginia,* 237.
[45] Henri Gaullieur, *Etudes Americaines* (Paris, 1891), 146.

the better classes of white men increasingly shrank from the practice and left it to the lower classes of both races. A contemporary, Philip A. Bruce, summed up the situation and white Virginians' attitudes in 1889:

> . . . illicit sexual commerce between the two races has diminished so far as to have almost ceased. . . . There was little improper intercourse between white men and negresses of the original type in the period before emancipation. . . . Even the former habit of cohabitating with mulattoes . . . is very rarely observed, now that the social relation between the negroes and the whites has been placed upon a different footing.
>
> [The white people] are very much opposed to any intercourse with the negro that acknowledges his social equality even temporarily; whoever among them, therefore is guilty of sexual commerce with a negress, disregards to that extent those principles which they consider essential to the permanent health and stability of their social life, and he falls in the general esteem in proportion.[46]

General Armstrong of Hampton Institute stated that, "As a result of their changed relations, the tendency to a [biological] mingling of the races seems much less strong than under the false conditions of slavery." [47]

General Armstrong was partly correct, but while the "false condition of slavery" had lent itself to racial intermingling and fear that interracial sexual relationships would constitute admission of social equality, there were other reasons for a marked decrease in the birth of mulatto babies. Three important factors were: (1) the increase in professional prostitution by Negro women, who found more acceptable economic opportunities to be severely limited, (2) the steady increase in the class of Negro women who, as they rose economically, educationally, and socially, rejected such proposals by white men, and (3) the limited but increased knowledge and popularization of contraception.

So far we have examined the attitudes of white Virginians toward the Negro in rather definite situations—the Negro in political office and on the police force, the Negro in society striving for equality of treatment, and the Negro in racial intermarriage. The lack of evi-

[46] Bruce, *Plantation Negro as a Freeman*, 53–55.
[47] Samuel C. Armstrong, Frederick Douglas, *et al.*, "The Future of the Negro," *North American Review*, CXXXIX (1884), 95–96.

dence makes it more difficult to say precisely what the whites thought of the Negroes generally as fellow human beings and citizens. Within the framework in which each race knew its place and remained in it, there was an aura of kindliness which softened the harsh realities of two races living side by side in two different worlds. Yet, "separation bred suspicion and hatred, fostered rumors, and misunderstanding, and created conditions that made extremely difficult any steps towards its reduction." [48] The two races "grew apart and soon began to be ignorant of the thought and life each of the other. The old intimate relation of the two was gone and nothing took its place. It was but natural that this ignorance should soon breed contempt and later hatred." [49]

Still there was in Virginia a more peaceful and outwardly pleasant racial relationship than those in many of the other Southern states. In March, 1871, the Harrisonburg *Old Commonwealth* proudly announced Virginia to be little addicted to Ku Klux Klan activity, while in other Southern states "hundreds of thousands are daily being deprived of their rights and subjected to every imaginable torture, and even death, at the hands of the mysterious Ku Klux." [50] In 1879 Campbell reported a rumor to the effect that "relations between blacks and whites are better in Virginia than in some other states." [51] About the same time, Thomas Wentworth Higginson reported that a condition of outward peace prevailed between the races, with no conspicuous outrages. [52] George W. Bagby, medical doctor turned literary romantic, observed during the later 1870's that relations between the two races were "far from hostile." [53] A much more positive statement for the period 1870–1874 was given to a U. S. Senate committee investigating Negro migration by a Negro named Henry Adams. Adams told the committee in 1880 that he was a member of an informal Negro group of some five-hundred persons who traveled through the South at their own expense and reported

---

[48] Franklin, "History of Racial Segregation in the U. S.," *Annals of the American Academy of Political and Social Science*, CCCIV (March, 1956), 8.
[49] W. D. Weatherford, "Race Relationship in the South," *Annals of the American Academy of Political and Social Science*, XLIV (1913), 166.
[50] Harrisonburg *Old Commonwealth*, March 22, 1871.
[51] Campbell, *White and Black*, 281.
[52] Higginson, "Some War Scenes Revisited," *Atlantic Monthly*, XLII (July, 1878), 6.
[53] George W. Bagby, *The Old Virginia Gentleman and Other Sketches*, edited and arranged by Ellen M. Bagby (Richmond, Va., 1948 edition), 288.

back to a sort of central organization in Shreveport, Louisiana, on Negro conditions as they found them. The Negroes, he affirmed, were receiving better treatment in Virginia than in any other Southern state. Next after Virginia, Adams ranked Kentucky and Tennessee.[54] Obviously referring to the mutual acceptance and easy, though guarded, familiarity between the races in Virginia, historian Edward A. Freeman wrote in 1883: "In the North it struck me that people tried to speak as well of the Negro as they could; in Virginia there seemed to be no such necessity."[55] The author of a recent study on the Negro in Richmond in the years 1880–1890 states that, "Racial relations in Richmond were far from good, but they were, on the whole, better than in most southern cities during the eighties."[56] Robert Russa Moton, successor to Booker T. Washington at Tuskegee Institute and a native of Prince Edward county, recorded in his autobiography how he was cordially received by whites as well as Negroes when he returned home from his first year as a student at Hampton Institute in 1886. Significantly, he noted that the older white people were friendlier than those of his own generation, who often went out of their way to avoid him and spoke only if Moton spoke first.[57] In Cumberland county, he found that the white people "were very kindly disposed toward . . . [the Negro] and anxious to sell land to coloured people."[58] Bitter and vindictive political relations did not extend to the personal sphere. For example, following the white supremacy campaign of 1873, amiable relations continued to exist. The Negro continued to look up to the whites and to depend upon them for employment, while the whites naturally turned to the Negroes for laborers.[59]

Several factors help to explain why Negro-white relations were often better in Virginia than elsewhere. The Old Dominion had long been accustomed to a considerable free Negro population, causing much less drastic social change following emancipation. Of the

[54] Aptheker, editor, *A Documentary History of the Negro People in the United States,* 718.

[55] Freeman, *Some Impressions of the U. S.,* 148.

[56] Thomas Eugene Walton, "The Negro in Richmond, 1880–1890," Unpublished M. A. Thesis (Howard University, 1950), 97.

[57] Robert Russa Moton, *Finding a Way Out: An Autobiography* (New York, 1920), 73.

[58] *Ibid.,* 99.

[59] Morton, *Negro in Virginia Politics,* 89.

roughly 260,000 free Negroes in the slave states in 1860, about half of them were in Virginia and Maryland.[60] Moreover, the relative lack of absentee landowning and the presence of few huge plantations, where hired overseers supervised the field gangs, led to a more intimate relationship between master and slave than was common farther south. Tobacco culture and a more diversified agricultural economy did not lend themselves to the mass production and impersonal methods of cotton culture. Tobacco and diversified farming demanded greater worker skill and care, so that many of the less intelligent and skilled slaves were "sold south" for the cotton plantations, which demanded little more than hands for chopping and picking cotton. Dr. Paul B. Barringer, Chairman of the Faculty of the University of Virginia, forthrightly claimed that the Negroes of Virginia were the mental and physical superiors of any others in the South as a result of Virginia's having been a "slave-breeding state" [*sic*] where only the progeny and culls were sold.[61]

All these factors, then, reduced the social and cultural barriers between the two races. The end result was often better relations than in other Southern states. The Negro who knew his place, stayed in it, and kept out of Republican politics, was unctuously rewarded by the press, especially in the obituary notices. Upon the death of Lemuel Bowser, who was just such an "old darkey," the *Dispatch* said:

> Lemuel Bowser, an old and much esteemed colored citizen of Richmond, died in this city on Monday night. There are but few colored men of Richmond who enjoyed more cordial esteem and universal respect than Lemuel Bowser did. A gentleman by association and raising, he treated all persons with the same respect he himself commanded, and, kind by nature, he won upon all with whom he was associated. He was a colored man who had under all circumstances preserved the kindly relations which existed between the white and colored people of Virginia in the olden time.[62]

[60] Arthur C. Cole, *The Irrespressible Conflict*, 1850–1865, vol. VII of *A History of American Life*, edited by Arthur M. Schlesinger and Dixon Ryan Fox (New York, 1934), 42.

[61] Paul B. Barringer, *The Sacrifice of a Race* (Raleigh, N. C., 1900), 17.

[62] Quoted in Taylor, "Negro in the Reconstruction of Virginia," *Journal of Negro History*, XI (1926), 247–248 from the *Richmond Daily Dispatch*, June 8, 1870.

Upon the death of Reverend Scott Gwathmey, the *Dispatch* said:

> He is represented as having been a good man and a faithful Christian, and was respected by all who knew him, and on more than one occasion he has given the colored people of Richmond some good advice. He eschewed politics and kept away from political meetings.[63]

The *Clarke Courier* of the lower Valley expressed similar sentiments upon the death of an aged former slave:

> He was a good servant, and when the right of franchise was given him he showed his appreciation of his master's kindness, and of the judgment of those among whom he was raised, by always voting the Conservative ticket.[64]

While the *Dispatch* was always in the vanguard of the white supremacists, other papers were equally conservative on the Negro problem. The Richmond *Enquirer* began the year 1871 by proclaiming its belief in the racial superiority of the whites over the blacks. The editor darkly warned that departure from this doctrine was in the interest of bad white men and would bring harm to good black men. He reminded the Negroes that their best friends were those who treated them as the majority of white Virginians treated them—*i.e.* as racial inferiors. Then he continued:

> Among all the people of the earth the colored people have hitherto found none that have so far advanced them in all things good for them as the Virginian people and those influenced by the Virginian people.[65]

Of two Negro state senators, the *Enquirer* jibed, under the heading, "Humors of Legislation—Sambo in the Senate":

> The Moss trooper from Buckingham [Frank Moss, born free, a farmer and a minister] and the little clam-baker from Elizabeth City, [Isaiah Lyons, from the North, died two weeks later] were in their seats in the Senate yesterday. . . . During the discussion on the tax bill the former . . . was laid on the flat of his back. He might possibly have got along better if it was something about a mule. 'Tis rare fun to listen to these descendants of Ham endeavoring to get out of their mouths the wonderful things that get into their heads.[66]

[63] Quoted in *Ibid.* from the Richmond *Daily Dispatch*, April 25, 1879.
[64] Reprinted in the Richmond *Daily Dispatch*, January 21, 1871.
[65] Richmond *Enquirer*, January 3, 1871.
[66] *Ibid.*, February 7, 1871.

Heading into the final days of the bitter campaign of 1883 which culminated in the Danville Riot,[67] a Valley newspaper declared with the finality and conviction of a poor-white Southside farmer: "The white race will rule, and that is the end to this question." [68] Reaffirming white supremacy, the Richmond *Weekly Dispatch* declared in 1890: "It is not in Caucasian human nature to acknowledge or to believe that 'a negro is as good as a white man'." And, "A thousand years of probation would leave a negro a negro." [69] Commenting on alleged unsatisfactory service by Negro volunteer troops in the Spanish-American War, the Lynchburg *Advance* asserted that, "Hereafter the inferiority of the race will not be denied in the North or in the South." [70] In the rabid *Daily Dispatch*, the anti-Negro campaign seemed to reach a peak in 1873. Upon the Senate's refusal to vote to open all branches of the army to the Negro, that newspaper declared: "In good time the negro will learn that all white men are, by reason of race, prejudiced against making associates of their colored brethren." [71]

The records of individuals also reflect the view that the Negro was racially inferior. In 1870, a white farmer of Halifax county wrote of the westward and southward migration of both races:

. . . a large number of Negroes & a good many whites have left this county for the South and West. I regret to see good white citizens leaving, but do not care how many Negroes go, for the way most of them [are] doing I consider them rather a curse than a helping to the country.[72]

On the other hand, James J. McDonald, writing about the Tidewater after the war, said that the whites were usually cooperative with industrious Negroes who desired to build homes, and sold them land on easy terms.[73]

It was gross exaggeration though, when the superintendent of the state's public schools, William Henry Ruffner, pronounced the Negro race to be without "moral character." Ruffner, a former slave-

[67] See above pp. 29–31.
[68] Harrisonburg *Old Commonwealth*, November 1, 1883.
[69] Richmond *Weekly Dispatch*, March 7, 1890.
[70] Lynchburg *Daily Advance*, November 26, 1898.
[71] Richmond *Daily Dispatch*, February 28, 1873.
[72] William Woodall to John Woodall, January 4, 1870. John Woodall Papers (Duke University Library).
[73] James J. McDonald, *Life in Old Virginia* (Norfolk, Va., 1907), 177.

holder and son of a slaveholding ancestry, declared: "The southern negroes are polite, amiable, quiet, orderly, and religious; and hence it is hard to believe that as a class they are without moral character. And yet such is the unhappy truth.[74] Ruffner was, of course, imposing his race's standards of moral conduct upon a race, which, only nine years earlier in servitude had rarely been encouraged by their masters in such conventions as formal marriage, marital fidelity, and other morés reflecting moral character and training.

In the same vein, Campbell found white Virginians defending the institution of slavery "without reserve," [75] and was told by a circuit court judge in Hampton that, "God made niggers different from white men, and nobody can make them the same." [76] In a lighter vein, Campbell related how, during a satirical play in Richmond, a "civil rights man" told of a "civil rights" barber shop in New York where both white and black were shaved. At this the audience appeared to be greatly amused.[77]

In the same city, and also in the late 1870's, the Scottish visitor C. B. Berry noted little respect by the white man for the Negro. He was told by a white man of the class who rarely left written records that, "They say the nigger's a man and a brother. Wall, I don't say he mayn't be somebody else's brother, but I reckon for sartin he ain't mine!" [78] Virginians of distinguished lineage, moreover, could declare against the danger of Africanization with the fervor of a poor-white in active competition with the Negro. "The master motive with me," wrote General William H. Payne, "is to save the state from Africanization. In such a storm I recognize the right of jettison, and to save the ship, will fling over every bale of goods and every Jonah." [79]

It remained for Camm Patteson, lawyer and graduate of the University of Virginia, former Confederate captain, and for eight years a member of his *Alma Mater's* Board of Visitors, to pen one of the darkest and most direful predictions on the future of race relations ever written in the South. Addressing H. St. George Tucker, in

---

[74] "Virginia School Report, 1874," *Annual Reports, 1873–1874*, p. 148.
[75] Campbell, *White and Black*, 290.
[76] *Ibid.*, 278.
[77] *Ibid.*, 289.
[78] C. B. Berry, *The Other Side: How it Struck Us* (London and New York, 1880), 91.
[79] General William H. Payne to J. W. Daniel, April 9, 1881. Daniel Papers.

1890, and promising to get out the congressional vote for the latter in
Cumberland county, Patteson wrote:

> I feel I am a pessimist about the negro; it is a solemn and serious
> question; my own idea is that a revolution is inevitable; not that there
> will be any actual *declared war* but that the horrible ideas which have
> been indubitably instilled in the heads of the negroes now for more
> than a quarter of a century are bound to bring forth bad fruit. I go
> so far as to believe this if the north should now turn and try to undo
> the infamous work it has done by relegating the negro to his proper
> sphere that still the revolution would come. They have taken the geneii
> [*sic*] out of the bottle and it is out of their power to put him back in it
> again. Certain events and causes always produce certain results. The
> mass of meanness and impudence heaped up in the negroes' head by
> twenty-five years work of old enemies can only find its vent in revolu-
> tion. It will commence very soon if such leaders as John M. Langston
> are allowed to excite them *i.e.* the negroes even more than they are.
> The white people will *not start it* but the negroes will. Like lightning
> it will spread from the Rio Grande due north to the Potomac; it will
> be short, sharp, and decisive and the Anglo Saxons of course will win
> but *not without a considerable struggle* (far more of a struggle than
> most people imagine) which will cost us severely; of course no good
> order loving law abiding white man in the South can contemplate such
> a result without sorrow, but we have the great consolation of know-
> ing that it was not of our seeking and that in the struggle we will be
> simply defending our homes, our firesides and our institutions. There
> is nowhere on earth in my honest opinion a population more law-
> abiding and more loyal to the United States of America than the
> population which resides in the Southern States of this union. The
> war between the states is with us an episode of the past. We again
> love the Union; we will never more secede and we have not the re-
> motest idea of being guilty of treason and I do not doubt but that when
> the negroes rise upon us with brutal and savage ferocity, that the
> people of the north will come to our rescue. It is barely possible that
> the splendid confederation of the Anglo Saxon race in the South may
> avert a civil war; this conservative confederation may possibly prevent
> it but this is my only hope. If the South had been peopled by the Latin
> race it would have long since come. To be forewarned is to be fore-
> armed. I advise you to boldly make the race issue. It is the true living
> issue; it must be settled before we can ever divide on economic ques-
> tions.[80]

[80] Camm Patteson to H. St. George Tucker, October 9, 1890. Tucker Family
Papers (University of North Carolina Library).

Dr. Paul B. Barringer told the Tri-State Medical Association of Virginia and the two Carolinas that the Negro was naturally a savage in whom the discipline of slavery had produced a temporary elevation. A generation later, by 1900, Dr. Barringer claimed that the Negro was slipping back into barbarism. Instead of trying academically to educate him out of barbarism, Barringer recommended an industrial or trade education for the Negro.[81] Barringer had met and corresponded with Booker T. Washington, the chief Negro expondent of "practical education" for his race.

Professor Richard Heath Dabney, like Barringer a member of the faculty of the University of Virginia, declared that, "All lawful measures should be taken to remove any removable cause of economic, social, or political competition between the races." [82] Another noted Virginian, George W. Bagby, declared that he and his friends agreed with the old Negroes who grew up under slavery and now spoke of the generation of Negroes born in freedom, as "sassy, triflin' and wuthless." [83]

Superior, haughty, intemperate, and unfair as the white attitudes were, they were nevertheless suffused by a kindly and tolerant if condescending air reminiscent of ante-bellum days. Exemplifying this strange but old relationship between the races in Virginia was an incident between a Negro and a "Marse Parmer" in the Lynchburg area. The Negro approached "Marse Parmer" and requested the loan of thirty dollars toward making up the first payment on some land he had just purchased. "Marse Parmer" promptly handed him the money, but accompanied it with the following:

> I don't want any note, for your note would not be worth the paper it is written on. I only want you to pay me back when you are able to do so; and if you get into trouble again, come to me and I will help you out. And I want you to understand that I do this because you are the same old nig.[ger] that you were in slavery times. The first time I meet you in the road and you fail to take off your hat, or treat me with respect you have always shown; or the first time you turn fool and go running after these new fangled ideas that a negro is as good as a white man— I want you to understand that I am done with you.

---

[81] Paul B. Barringer, *The American Negro: His Past and Future* (Raleigh, N. C., 1900), 23.

[82] Quoted in Editorial, "Two Southern Views," *Outlook*, LXIX (November 30, 1901), 810.

[83] Bagby, *The Old Virginia Gentleman and Other Sketches*, 284.

The Negro pocketed the money, and as was expected of him, profusely thanked "Marse Parmer" and assured him that he would remain "the same old nigger." [84]

Similarly paternal, Dr. Barringer, who two years previously had pronounced the Negro as being naturally a savage slipping back into barbarism,[85] wrote to the editor of *Outlook* magazine pleading for $16,000 to build a ward for colored patients at the University of Virginia Hospital. At the time, both white and black patients were crowded into the hospital administration building, with Negroes on the first floor and whites on the second, a reversal of the usual order. Funds had been promised for the building of a white ward as a memorial, but Barringer said none was forthcoming for a colored ward. After a visit to Charlottesville, the editor had nothing but praise for what the University Hospital was doing for Negro patients.[86] Indicative of white concern for "their colored citizens" was Governor Kemper's address to the General Assembly in 1874, in which he called for moral and educational development of the Negro and for mutual aid in all lines of progress of the two races, but with continued social division of the races.[87]

Philip Alexander Bruce candidly admitted that white acceptance of Negro progress in whatever areas, was born of a sense of utilitarianism—a sort of, "If we have to have them let's make them as useful to us as possible," approach. Particularly was this attitude true in regard to the schooling of Negroes.[88] In spite of emancipation, many white Southerners felt that the Negro still belonged to them. Twenty-one years after the war, a Virginian piously and paternalistically declared:

> Every true Southern man and woman has a sincere affection for the negroes, not so much because of their virtues, which, however, are fully recognized, as because they did once in form, and do still in fact belong to us: they are our people, they are an element in our society, they are in the habit of serving our needs, and we [are] in the habit of serving theirs. . . . You will please pardon us, but we have a sort of love for our negroes.[89]

[84] Richmond *Daily Dispatch*, September 14, 1871.
[85] Barringer, *American Negro*, 23.
[86] Editor, "A Pathetic Appeal," *Outlook*, LXVIII (August 17, 1901), 903.
[87] Morton, *Negro in Virginia Politics*, 90.
[88] Bruce, *Plantation Negro as a Freeman*, 58.
[89] Davis, "Negro in the South," *Forum*, I (April, 1886), 132–133.

There is no reason to doubt the writer's sincerity and conviction. It was just such genuine feelings as these which occasionally had softened the institution of slavery. But the memory of that old relationship made the very thought of social equality repugnant to the whites. A noted scholar, Georgia's Joseph Le Conte, declared that, "The whites, I believe, desire earnestly—more earnestly than can be well imagined by those at a distance—the real best interests of the blacks." [90] What those best interests were, however, were to be determined by the whites; such interests did not include exercise of rights or privileges commonly construed as social equality by those same whites. More than a decade after the beginning of the adoption of Jim Crow laws and disfranchisement by the new constitution of 1902, a study of Negro economic development in the Tidewater concluded: "The Negroes of . . . the Tidewater counties, in fact all over the state, have been greatly encouraged in their efforts to accumulate property and to become substantial citizens by the best element of native white people." [91]

Camm Patteson, as the century ended, optimistically played the old note of kindly paternalism, with the Negro in his place:

> The great battle for supremacy is practically over, and they [*i.e.* the Negroes] have fallen into a mediocre state which seems to content them, and never again, as a class is it probable that they will attempt to override the Anglo-Saxon rule . . . it behooves us to treat him with justice and kindness and conciliation, and they undoubtedly are so treated. Their rights of personal security, personal liberty and private property are everywhere respected in the South, and it is done from a feeling of kindness, which is the result of association.
>
> We know him, and he knows that we know him; we are disposed to condone his petty violations of right, and, as a rule, we always help him when he is in distress, and we do it from true principles of friendship.
>
> I conclude this article with the prediction that the negro has given us more trouble in the past than he will ever again give us in the future. The large homogeneous white population of the South will dominate him, but they will treat him with kindness and justice. . . .

---

[90] Joseph Le Conte, *The Race Problem in the South*, in *Man and the State—Studies in Applied Sociology*, XXIX (New York, May 1, 1892), 364.

[91] T. C. Walker, "Development [of the Negro] in the Tidewater Counties of Virginia," *Annals of the American Academy of Political and Social Science*, XLIX (1913), 31.

The Cavalier understands his nature; the Puritan does not . . . as time passes, the negro will become more contented when he finds, as he surely will, that he must always occupy a position subordinate to the white race. We of the South will not only do the negro no injustice, but, on the contrary, we will generously aid him in his aspirations for a higher and better existence. All we ask as to this question from our Northern brethren is to let us alone. Of all the people in the world, we are the best suited to solve the problem of his destiny. . . .[92]

Since Virginia, of all the English colonies in America, had most nearly copied the seventeenth and eighteenth century English ideal of a rural aristocracy, it is not surprising that later white Virginians held ideas about the inferiority of other and lesser races similar to those held by some people in nineteenth century England. And, though reference was rarely made to it as such, undoubtedly white Virginians were influenced by the Social Darwinian theories of Herbert Spencer and his disciples. Widespread acceptance by much of the North of the tenets of Social Darwinism was a contributing factor to the *rapprochement* between North and South, as the latter watched the North embrace ideas it had long held about the inferiority of the Negro.

Frequently white Virginians found their attitudes toward the colored race supported and buttressed by their English cousins. In 1872, the *Dispatch* proudly reprinted the following judgment of the Virginia Negro by an unnamed Englishman:

The negroes, whatever they may become, are at present ignorant in the extreme, and totally unfit for social equality with educated people, whether black or white. By all means "educate the negro," but while he is ignorant do not place him in a false position by making him your social equal. To do the black man justice, he does not desire to obtrude himself in circles for which he is unfitted. Sambo is an excellent fellow in his own place, and as a rule he greatly prefers to occupy that place.[93]

Historian Edward A. Freeman warned white Americans that, "You may give him the rights of citizenship by law; you cannot make him

---

[92] Camm Patteson, *The Young Bachelor* (Lynchburg, Virginia, 1900), 105–108.

[93] Reprinted in the Richmond *Daily Dispatch*, May 2, 1872, from the New York *Commercial Advertiser*.

the equal, the real fellow, of citizens of European descent." [94] Another English visitor observed more accurately:

> Since the artificial connection between the two races was severed by the abolition of slavery they [i.e. the white and black races] seem to have each fallen back within themselves, and left a yawning gulf between, across which it is not easy to imagine that even in their remotest future any bridge can stretch. [95]

Samuel Reynolds Hole, Dean of Rochester Cathedral, noted how white Virginians at the University of Virginia defended the institution of slavery, while some of them even maintained that the Negroes were happier enslaved. With characteristic English understatement, Hole wrote that he saw no probability of amalgamation of the white and black races. [96]

The most noted of the English observers was James Lord Bryce, whose *American Commonwealth* soon became a classic. Though Bryce generally referred only to the "Southern Negro," not the "Virginia Negro," his observations are still valuable here. Bryce was struck by the way in which Southern whites had thrown up a social barrier against the Negro since the war. Still, among the educated and upper-class whites he noted no sense of hostility toward the Negro as a race. But this was not the case with the poorer whites, those who were in economic competition with the Negro and feared most for their own poor position in society. A Virginian told Bryce that, "Our whites don't molest the negroes so long as the negroes don't presume!" Like numerous others, Bryce noted that there was little intercourse between the races except in domestic service. [97]

---

[94] Freeman, *Impressions of the U. S.*, 144.

[95] Anonymous, "A Social Study of Our Oldest Colony," *Littell's Living Age*, CLXI (1884), 370–371.

[96] Samuel Reynolds Hole, *A Little Tour in America* (London and New York, 1895), 225–228. Hole's reactions to the University provide a sidelight on Virginia history. He was not very much impressed by the Greek revival architecture of the University, finding the Rotunda pleasing but the dormitories small and low. He found the undergraduates who occupied them bright and cheery and the professors kind and hospitable. Hole felt himself "more fortunate than Emerson, of whom we read that he went to lecture to the literary societies of the University of Virginia, and that there was so much noise that he could not make himself heard, and, after contending with the din for half an hour, concluded." After his lecture, while conversing with one of the "Dons of the University" on the classics in general and on the superiority of the Greek language over the English, he was interrupted by a pleasant voice announcing: "Dean Hole, we know that you are a sportsman, and we propose to have a special meet of the hounds to-morrow morning in your honour."—pp. 229–230.

[97] Bryce, *American Commonwealth*, II, pp. 504–505.

Bryce's most cogent comment was reserved for the status of the small class of cultured and educated Negroes in the South, for in that group's isolation lay the most convincing evidence that white Southerners refused to meet the Negro as an equal in any area, because he was a Negro, not because he was only recently released from slavery and had hence not learned the morés and proprieties of white society. Bryce found the educated Negroes to be

> as little in contact with their white neighbors as are the humblest coloured labourers, perhaps even less. No prospect is open to them, whatever wealth or culture they may acquire, of finding an entrance into white society, and they are made to feel in a thousand ways that they belong to a caste condemned to perpetual inferiority.[98]

That this condition was a fact, a native Virginian admitted when he wrote: "The nearer the negro approaches to the white man's standard of civilization, the less love there is between them." [99]

French observers generally were more critical than the English. George Nestler Tricoche pointed out in 1894, that the South had no monopoly upon anti-Negro sentiment and cited as evidence a long list of racial incidents from Boston to Washington. In Massachusetts, he pointed out, Negro doctors, lawyers, and clergymen were limited to serving their own race. Boston merchants would not employ Negroes. In Asbury Park, New Jersey, Negroes could not frequent the public beaches at the same hours as the whites. In Brooklyn, New York, and Washington, the Y.M.C.A. was closed to Negro membership. In Pittsburgh, an extremely lightskinned mulatto child was turned out of school because of "mixed blood." [100] The charge of "mixed blood," said Tricoche, "remains an argument without response in the United States in spite of all doctrines of equality." [101] And if liberal Northerners came to live in the South, they soon laid aside those feelings toward the Negro and embraced the opinions of native white Southerners.[102]

Most observers, whether native or foreign, were content merely to record what they saw. Few looked beneath the white Southerner's stereotyped prejudice or sought the true reasons for the accepted code of conduct between the two races. Fewer still condemned what

---

[98] *Ibid.*, II, p. 508.
[99] Thomas, *Virginia Constitutional Convention and its Possibilities*, 17.
[100] Tricoche, *La Question Des Noirs Aux Etats-Unis*, 16–17.
[101] *Ibid.*, 146–147.
[102] *Ibid.*, 13–14.

they saw. But there were some who condemned, only to have the finger of scorn pointed at them by the conservative white South on the defensive. Criticism apparently failed to soften race attitudes of Southern whites, because they sought the harder to justify the existence of the two separate worlds, which increasingly became the mark of the South.

The discerning and critical Tricoche charged that white Southerners treated the Negroes as inferiors for two reasons—one the fancied reason and the other the unvoiced real reason. The fancied reason was fear of being ruled by the Negro. The real reason was "the desire to keep the Negro population in a state of semi-servitude where it is at present found." [103] On the other hand, DuBois claimed that the economic importance of certain Negroes in Farmville, such as teachers and preachers, brought many white men to address them as "mister" and to raise their hats to those Negroes' wives.[104]

Stripping paternalism bare of all its kindliness, a white Virginian who offered three solutions to the Negro problem—segregation, subordination, or extermination[105]—frankly stated, in 1901: "The negro that the white man likes best is the one who does his menial work best for the least pay." [106] The agricultural historian, Lewis Cecil Gray, pointed out in 1912 that the whites did not encourage Negro thrift, as to do so was to remove the Negro's dependence upon them. The Negro, argued Gray, would not be encouraged to put out a garden or to "raise meat." On the other hand, the white man might pay the Negro's fine in order to tighten his hold on him.[107] Gray wisely declared: "There is too little desire to deal with the problem in the spirit of improving the negro and making him a better citizen. Indeed, this spirit is impossible so long as the present separation between the races exists." [108]

Of all the native and contemporary critics of Virginia and the South, perhaps the most discerning was the now nearly-forgotten Lewis H. Blair. He criticized his land not because he was quarrelsome, or a publicity-seeker, or even an idealist. He was a realist who

---

[103] *Ibid.*, 13.
[104] DuBois, "Negroes of Farmville," *Bulletin of the Dept. of Labor*, III (1898), 22.
[105] Thomas, *Virginia Constitutional Convention and its Possibilities*, 18.
[106] *Ibid.*, 20.
[107] Gray, *Southern Agriculture . . . and the Negro Problem*, 97.
[108] *Ibid.*, 99.

sought to diagnose the social and economic ailments of Virginia and the South and to make them known that they might be treated. He was also a pragmatist, as the very title of his book shows: *The Prosperity of the South Dependent Upon the Elevation of the Negro.* Declaring the South to be a "veritable land of caste," which in spite of all the social gradations, saw all white men grouped into one superior caste,[109] Blair wrote:

> It is doubtless very gratifying to our baser nature to control absolutely the actions of a whole class of our fellow-creatures; but the enjoyment is suicidal, and it will end in our moral enfeeblement and in our material impoverishment, for ruin must follow communities that persistently degrade any large portion of its [*sic*] citizens.[110]

On political equality, Blair maintained that, "The South will look in vain for prosperity as long as it abridges the right of voting of any class of its citizens.[111] On paternalism and the alleged genuine kindness and sympathy for the Negro, Blair bluntly declared:

> . . . most of our kindness to the negroes proceeds from the standpoint of condescension, and of assumed caste superiority, and we expect it to be received with humility and from a feeling of acknowledged caste inferiority; and if not so received by the negroes, they are thought impudent . . . and the fountain of our kindness soon dries up.[112]

Again reminding the white South of the price it was paying for the racial codes on which it insisted, Blair warned: "Oligarchy, caste, vassalage are the regnant spirit in the greater portion of the South, and no country can prosper under their weight."[113]

George W. Cable asked: "Must the average mental and moral caliber of the whole Negro race in America equal that of the white race, before *any* Negro in a Southern State is entitled to the civil and political standing decreed to all [white] citizens of the United States except the criminal and insane?"[114]

To these cries few listened; and fewer still heeded them. There

---

[109] Blair, *Prosperity of the South Dependent Upon the Elevation of the Negro*, 50–51.

[110] *Ibid.*, 84–85.

[111] *Ibid.*, 86.

[112] *Ibid.*, 116.

[113] *Ibid.*, 117.

[114] George W. Cable, "A Simpler Negro Question," *Forum*, VI (Dec., 1888), 402.

was no desire to face the Negro problem and solve it. It was easier to legislate away both his political and civil rights and then deny that a problem existed. While progress had been made and hope for the Negro had once glittered brightly, there was no denying that immediately after the Civil War, Virginia and the rest of the South had begun the "erection of a new [social and economic] structure upon the basis of the old philosophy. By the turn of the twentieth century that adjustment had become fixed in a biracial social and economic order." [115]

---

[115] Guion Griffis Johnson, "The Idealogy of White Supremacy, 1877–1910," *Essays in Southern History*, Fletcher M. Green, editor—*The James Sprunt Studies in History and Political Science*, XXXI (Chapel Hill, N. C., 1949), 135.

Chapter 7

Some Negro Attitudes

THE attitude of the Negro toward his new role in Southern society as it emerged is difficult to ascertain. Few Negroes were literate enough to leave written records. In addition, many of the newly-emancipated Negroes continued to follow the slavery-ingrained habit of masking their real feelings from the white man who once owned and still largely controlled them. Fortunately, there was a small but vital Negro press. The best known Negro newspaper in Virginia was the Richmond *Planet*. Founded in 1883, the *Planet* was edited by the militant and fearless John W. Mitchell, who made it a literal "anti-lynch journal." Such a paper was indeed needed, for the white-owned and edited papers were not to be relied upon in reporting the facts of a lynching.[1] Mitchell's single-mindedness of purpose served, however, to prevent the *Planet's* presenting anything like as complete a chronicle of the Negro in Virginia as it might have done. And the extreme militancy of Mitchell's entire approach served only to place his paper at the opposite extreme from the Richmond *Dispatch*. The Negro press also included the Richmond *Virginia Star* and the Petersburg *Lancet*, but more genuinely informative was the *Southern Workman*, published monthly by the Hampton Institute. Negroes also occasionally found press outlets through Northern magazines. A final source for revealing what the Negro thought were the writings of white observers who recorded what the Negro occasionally told them and what they saw.

Throughout the period, the older Negroes paid greater deference to their former masters than the rising youths who often showed deep resentment at the inferior status accorded them. Some carried on daily life under a mask of resignation, but perhaps a majority adapted their lives to the position accepted for them by their conservative leader, Booker T. Washington. But the intelligent, literate Negro held an utterly different view of the meaning of social equality from that held by most of the whites. The Richmond *Dispatch* observed with a good deal of truth, in 1872, that "all acts of kindness

---

[1] Bryce, *American Commonwealth*, II, p. 506.

from the whites are treated by them [*i.e.* the Negroes] as designing." [2] To the editor of this newspaper, the Negro exhibited an un-
duly surly and distrustful attitude toward white men when they
really tried to help him.[3] The venerable Democrat, John Goode,
noted in his memoirs, that, "The young men and women of the
black race who have grown up since the war seem to cherish a feeling
of animosity toward the whites in their midst." [4] Like Goode, Lord
Bryce noted that the generation of Negroes reared after the war was
much less friendly toward the whites than were former slaves.[5] In
addition to these obvious and natural responses from the young and
the old Negroes, one must consider that white acts of kindness toward Negroes *were* often designing and aimed at making the Negro
even more dependent upon the white man than he was already.[6]

An English visitor found the Virginia Negro, in 1884, to be
"neither rude nor arrogant, but . . . rather by nature civil, and
generally ready to render any small service over and above his regular work that may be required of him." [7] But, he continued:

> The negro . . . in spite of the protestations that run smoothly from
> his glib tongue, does not as a rule care a straw for the good opinion of
> the white employing class, though his manner towards such is usually
> that of a servant to his master and his feelings anything but un-
> friendly. Of the bad opinion of his own race, however, he lives in
> pious dread. . . .[8]

White sympathizers in the South who would fight for the Negro's
cause were few, but always foremost among them were Lewis H.
Blair of Virginia and George W. Cable of Louisiana. Going to the
real heart of the injustice of inflexible and apparently permanent,
racial discrimination, Cable declared that that policy became ever
harder for the Negro to bear as he slowly lifted himself to the white
man's standards of education, morality, and conduct. "The farther
he rises above . . . [his former] life . . . the more he is galled

---

[2] Richmond *Daily Dispatch*, May 3, 1872.
[3] *Ibid.*, March 14, 1872.
[4] John Goode, *Recollections of a Lifetime by John Goode of Virginia* (New
York and Washington, 1906), 225.
[5] Bryce, *American Commonwealth*, II, p. 506.
[6] Gray, *Southern Agriculture . . . and the Negro Problem*, 97.
[7] Anonymous, "A Social Study of Our Oldest Colony," *Littell's Living Age*,
CLXI (1884), 369.
[8] *Ibid.*, 371.

and tormented with ignominious discriminations made against him as a public citizen, both by custom and by law. . . ." [9] Bluntly replying to white charges of Negro surliness, suspicion, and distrust, Blair declared, in 1889:

> The negroes are against us simply because we treat them not as citizens, but as creatures who have no rights we are bound to respect. [10]
> . . . the whites, instead of having six millions of friends and co-workers in prosperity, as they should have if they showed only a willingness to elevate the negro, have that number of secret foes in their midst. [11]

There were many white Virginians who, while perhaps glad to be free of the burden of slavery, nevertheless not only naively believed that the Negroes were better off enslaved, but also held that the Negroes preferred their former condition. With a combination of romanticism, pride, and pathos, Virginians would relate how old Negroes begged to be allowed to return to their former masters' homes, because, as one ex-slave claimed, there were "too many niggers and Yankees in Richmond." [12] And Virginia newspapers were always glad to reprint items like the following:

> The colored man here [Richmond] seemingly entertains the same views on the question of social equality as his white brother, and he does not appear at all willing that the situation should be turned upside down. [13]
> In the South there are schools for colored children . . . and the colored schools are taught by colored teachers.
> In the North colored children may get an education, may fit themselves for teaching, but there are no schools here for them to teach.
> [In the] South . . . negro character is understood, and . . . negroes of integrity, education, and ability are appreciated and respected by the better class of whites.
> The sober, industrious, and enterprising negro has more opportunities for advancement in the South than in the North. [14]

---

[9] George W. Cable, "What Shall the Negro Do?" *Forum*, V (August, 1888), 628.
[10] Blair, *Prosperity of the South Dependent Upon the Elevation of the Negro*, 83.
[11] *Ibid.*, 120.
[12] Bagby, *The Old Virginia Gentleman and Other Sketches*, 288.
[13] Reprinted in the Richmond *Daily Dispatch*, October 9, 1886, from the New York *Times*.
[14] Reprinted in the Lynchburg *Daily Advance*, October 21, 1897, from the New York *Age* (Negro).

Such statements, of course, were only clichés or half-truths. For example, almost all of the alleged educational and most of the economic opportunities lay in a segregated or separate, Negro world. Many Negroes, including some Negro leaders, did, for one reason or another, play a role of ingratiation and propitiation. But the vast majority of them perhaps merely tried to adjust so as to survive.

In answer to white charges of possible Negro rule, Lewis H. Blair replied:

> . . . how do the negroes act in the so-called black counties? Do they say to the whites, as the whites say to them, "No whites need apply"? No; . . . they give the whites about every sheriff, every treasurer, every commissioner of the revenue, every county and every circuit court clerk, and they content themselves with being justices of the peace, janitors and such like. Whatever their other defects, the negroes, as a rule, have sense enough to select for officeholders the best whites they can find in their own party, and in default of them, they select the best Democrats attainable.[15]

In the old spirit of looking up to the "best white people," a correspondent of the *Southern Workman* wrote, in 1888:

> In nine cases out of ten where difficulties occur between the races, they are brought on by that class of whites who think and act that a colored person hasn't any rights which a white man is bound to respect.
>
> If we had to deal with our old masters only, a much better state of affairs would exist to-day in the South.[16]

Increasingly the attitude of the Negro became one of hopeless resignation. The best expression of this attitude is from the pen of the Reverend Robert Davis of the African Methodist Episcopal Church, Rocky Mount, Virginia, written on August 29, 1890.

> We held quarterly meeting at Rocky Mount, Va., August 23–28th. . . .
>
> Last November this town was set on fire and twenty-six stores and dwellings were burned. George Early, William Brown, Bird Woods and Nannie Woods, all colored were charged with the burning. They were tried at the December term of the county court and sentenced to be hanged August 24th '90. Our quarterly conference occurred on

---

[15] Blair, *Prosperity of the South Dependent Upon the Elevation of the Negro,* 114–115.

[16] L. L. I. to the Editor, Hampton *Southern Workman,* August, 1888.

the same day. George Early and Bird Woods were hanged. William Brown and Nannie Woods will be hanged September 19th. The authorities seem to like the fun so well that instead of making one do all, they got the governor to respite the other two till September 19th.

Our people were at a loss what to do. Some said the quarterly meeting would not go on and then came to me to know about it. I told them yes, the meeting would go on just the same. I told them that the white people had been hanging our people for nearly three hundred years and it was not worth while [*sic*] for me to stop my meeting. So we went on and had more people present than ever before. We prayed, sang and preached as though no one had been hanged, notwithstanding the occasion was one of great solemnity—an awful time. These men faced death boldly and in a firm voice protested their innocence, and said, 'It was hard to die for an infamous offense of which they were not guilty.' How long, oh Lord, with greatest depths will colored men have to stand on the scaffolds of the South and plead for their innocence in vain? O, Lord, that thy judgments may sit on our oppressors. Our people generally believe that these parties were innocent, hence it has inspired deep unrest and dissatisfaction among the colored people here.[17]

On the gallows one of the condemned men—presumably William Brown—confessed that he had lied in giving testimony which convicted Nannie Woods. He admitted that she was in no way connected with the crime. Governor McKinney then commuted her punishment to imprisonment for life. After five years of imprisonment she was pardoned by Governor O'Ferrall almost immediately upon his coming to office. Of the case, O'Ferrall reportedly declared, "I have never read of a case in which a greater wrong was done." [18]

A few Negroes like Booker T. Washington of Tuskegee Institute, chastised their own race for its failings and impatience and cautioned it to go slow. Professor Kelly Miller of Howard University warned that, "No people have ever been lifted into all of their rights and privileges by legislative fiat. . . . The Negro must learn to labor and to wait." [19] In 1900, another writer in the *Southern Workman* (probably colored) declared that,

---

[17] Copy of in Aptheker, ed., *Documentary History of the Negro People in the U. S.*, 748–749, as taken from the *Christian Recorder*, September 11, 1890. Strangely, no white newspaper in the state even reported the incident, when it was their usual practice to report in every detail executions of both white and black. It did, however, take place.

[18] Richmond *Planet*, February 9, 1894.

[19] Hampton *Southern Workman*, December, 1898.

. . . the Negro has only himself to blame for much that he attributes to prejudice and unrelenting hate. . . . His destiny is largely in his own hands and he ought to know it. . . . [Where the Negro comes in contact with the white man] what kind of impression does he make. . . . At all these points he is woefully defective and has made a bad reputation for himself. And this explains in part the apparent growth of unfavorable public opinion.

Only by education and the elevation of morals and economic status, maintained the writer, could the Negro "accelerate social evolution" and make himself a satisfactory member of society.[20]

The next year, 1901, Booker T. Washington, in a conciliatory mood, wrote to Dr. Paul B. Barringer, the white supremacist who had declared the Negro to be naturally a savage: [21]

Since we met in Chicago I have thought much concerning your earnest words, and the more I consider what you have said the more I am sure that on the vital points connected with the elevation of our race, there is not so much difference between us as I feared there was. . . . I feel that in working together we can accomplish much towards the solution of the problem which is so dear to the hearts of all of us.[22]

Despite this mounting mood of compromise, the whites were apparently still convinced that social equality was the ultimate goal of the Negro. But to the two groups the term meant different things. To the whites, it had a deeply personal meaning: the presence of Negroes in one's most private circle and the inevitability of intermarriage. To the Negro, it meant only the recognized right to equal and indiscriminate enjoyment of the services of public establishments, amusements, and transportation. It meant treatment as an individual in personal matters such as entertainment in one's home and intermarriage. It also meant acceptance or rejection on the basis of education, attainment, economic importance, the same criteria used by the whites in determining who their social associates would be. Time and time again the Negro defined his position, but to no avail.

Immediately following passage of the Civil Rights Act of 1875, the Negroes of Gordonsville called a bi-racial meeting in order to make known their views on the new measure. An Elder Barnett,

---

[20] *Ibid.*, October, 1900.
[21] Barringer, *American Negro*, 23.
[22] Booker T. Washington to Paul B. Barringer, March 13, 1901. Barringer, *The Natural Bent: The Memoirs of Dr. Paul B. Barringer* (Chapel Hill, N. C., 1949), 264.

speaking for the Negroes, told the whites that the Negroes had no intention of invading places they were not wanted. Said the *Shenandoah Valley* of the meeting: "The utmost order and good feeling prevailed." [23]

A Negro speaker in Washington, D. C., aptly expressed what she said were her race's views on social equality:

The matter of social equality will be, and ought to be, left to individual preferences . . . we are not contending for this sort of recognition from our white friends. . . . We do not practice unrestricted equality among ourselves. . . . We are not objecting because we are excluded from the social whirl. . . . We can take care of ourselves in a purely social way. But when their prejudices make them set up individious distinctions and discriminations in public licensed dining halls, hotels and places of amusement, make them want to exclude us from the avenues of remunerative employment, the commercial world, and make them deny to the most cultured and aspiring among us admission to their best professional schools, schools of art, their professional, scientific and literary associations, we think it a hardship which we, as loyal American citizens, ought not to be compelled to endure. [24]

Through the pages of *Forum* magazine a Negro minister named J. C. Price denied that in demanding his political and civil rights the Negro was at the same time demanding social equality. [25] "The position that political and civil equality carries with it . . . [social equality as] a consequence is contrary to the experience of all men, and especially to that of southern [white] men." The Reverend Price went on to point out that the poor white man, who enjoyed political and civil equality, did not enjoy social equality and no one feared that he ever would. [26] Warming to his subject, the Rev. Price continued:

If a Negro lays claim to what the law of the land guarantees to him, is he seeking social equality? No; he asks only that which is his already, and which he ought not to be compelled to seek. When a person of Negro descent enters a first-class car or restaurant, or seeks a decent stateroom on a steamer, he does not do it out of a desire to be with white people. He is seeking simply comfort, and not the companion-

[23] New Market *Shenandoah Valley*, March 19, 1875.
[24] Quoted in Edward Ingle, "The Negro in the District of Columbia," *Johns Hopkins University Studies in Historical and Political Science*, XI (1893), 62–63.
[25] Reverend J. C. Price, "Does the Negro Seek Social Equality?" *Forum*, X (January, 1891), 558.
[26] *Ibid.*, 562.

ship, or even the presence of whites. . . . When a train stops for
refreshments, and the Negro enters a dining room, he does not go
there because he is seeking social contact with the whites, but because
he is hungry. Notice the inconsistency involved in this matter. A train
stops twenty minutes for dinner. A Negro nurse walks into the dining
room and no one says a word to her. A well-dressed, intelligent
colored woman, with a famishing child, is refused accommodation, on
the assumption that she is seeking social equality. This same inconsistency is manifested on cars, on steamboats, and in other places of
public accommodation.

The Negro does not seek among other races what he does not have
in his own. There is no social equality among Negroes. . . . Culture,
moral refinement, and material possessions make a difference among
colored people as they do among whites. . . .

There is, to my mind, a very patent reason why this social bugbear
is thus brought into the discussion of the race problem. The same
cause brings it into prominence in political campaigns in many parts
of the South. . . . Every conceivable thing has been done to array
the [white] American people against granting the Negro his constitutional rights; and every struggle in the field of reason has ultimately
resulted, with the more thoughtful [white] people, in a triumph of the
Negro. The social-equality question is now brought forward because
it is considered the most effective stroke of policy for uniting the
Anglo-Saxon people of the country against the manhood rights of the
Negro.[27]

The militant Richmond *Planet* reiterated the Rev. Price's distinction
between political and civil rights and social equality:

As a matter of fact the colored people of the South have no desire for
social equality. . . .

We are however in favor of civil rights and equality before the law.
To that end, all persons enjoying public franchises, should be made to
extend to the public irrespective of color the same treatment for the
same money, and color and caste should form no part of the transac-
tion.[28]

Lord Bryce observed that Negro spokesmen had declared
through the press that they did not seek social equality with the
whites. They declared, explained Bryce,

[27] *Ibid.*, 562–564.
[28] Richmond *Planet*, April 6, 1895.

that they are quite willing to build up a separate society of their own, and seek neither intermarriage nor social intercourse, but that what they do ask is equal opportunity in business, the professions, and politics, equal recognition of the worth of their manhood, and a discontinuance of the social humiliations they are now compelled to endure.[29]

The astute French observer, Tricoche, also denied that the Negro was looking for social equality. This, he maintained, was only a common charge made by the whites whenever the Negro attempted to exercise his civil rights or to enjoy some of the comforts and better things of society.[30]

Thus, social equality had become a bugbear to be manipulated at will by the politicians and used by the white population at large as the final argument for keeping the Negro in an inferior position. By 1903, the Negro novelist, Charles W. Chesnutt, could note that Negro rights had sunk to their lowest point in thirty-five years, with race prejudice stronger and more uncompromising than ever before.[31] It was no wonder that David F. St. Clair, white, returning to the South in 1899 after an absence of ten years, found instead of the "old-time darkey . . . a self-conscious colored man, less optimistic, less mirthful, less improvident, perhaps more morose, more melancholy, and with a more acute sense of pain and suffering."[32]

Out of the widening worlds of Negro and white had come a fundamental misunderstanding of what was really meant by the term "social equality." Logic and technical correctness were on the side of the Negro definition, and there is no reason for believing that what they sought was, in reality, any different from the social equality sought by all white men—equality of treatment in public places and social acceptance or rejection upon the basis of individual merit, virtue, and taste. This misunderstanding and false interpretation of motive was but another of the unfortunate products born of the creation and maintenance of two separate worlds, between which there was no true communication.

[29] Bryce, *American Commonwealth*, II, p. 509.
[30] Tricoche, *La Question Des Noirs Aux Etats-Unis*, 11.
[31] Cited in Woodward, *Strange Career of Jim Crow*, 80–81.
[32] Quoted in Editorial, "The Negro in the New South," *Outlook*, LXIII (October 7, 1899), 284.

Chapter 8
Evolving White Attitudes toward Negro Education

VIRGINIANS, white and black, were aware that if the former slaves and their descendants were to fit themselves for the social and political responsibilities of free men in a free society, the tool of education must be placed at their disposal. By virtue of both the educational and moral denials suffered under slavery and passed on to descendants, only schools for all, or public schools, could aid greatly in the removal of those deficiencies.

Thus, in the beginning, there seems to have been no great opposition by the whites to the education of Negroes—with two qualifications. The principle of public education *per se* was not popular enough in Virginia to result in a state-supported system of public schools till 1870. Also, while the Negro might be educated at public expense, he should not be educated out of his place. Hence, in the white, popular mind, the ability to read and write was generally regarded as sufficient. A sort of practical realism such as, "If we have to have them let's make them as useful to us as possible," led white Virginians to accept a modicum of public education for the Negro.[1] But from the first, there was little if any evidence that white Virginians would voluntarily accept mixed schools, even at some vague future date. Nor were the separate Negro schools at any time equal to white schools in respect to proportionate numbers, physical facilities, or teacher salaries.[2] Shortage of Negro teachers often made necessary the staffing of Negro schools with white teachers and principals, to the general dissatisfaction of Negroes.[3] Often white teachers were used even though Negro teachers were available.[4] As

---

[1] Bruce, *Plantation Negro as a Freeman*, 58.
[2] William Henry Brown, *The Education and Economic Development of the Negro in Virginia*, Phelps-Stokes Fellowship Paper of the University of Virginia (Charlottesville, Va., 1923), 53; *Nation*, XIX (November 12, 1874), 316; Pearson, *Readjuster Movement in Virginia*, 61; Martin, "Negro Disfranchisement in Virginia," *Howard University Studies in the Social Sciences*, I, p. 94.
[3] "Virginia School Report, 1883," *Annual Reports, 1882–1883*, p. 141; Writers Project of the WPA, *Negro in Virginia*, 270.
[4] Taylor, "Negro in the Reconstruction of Virginia," *Journal of Negro History*, XI (1926), 402.

late as 1938 [*sic*] eight of the sixteen Negro schools in Richmond still had white principals![5]

As the century wore on, white attitudes continued to harden against education for the Negroes despite the brief boon of Readjuster legislation in the early 1880's. The Underwood Constitution, ratified in 1869, had required the General Assembly to establish a state tax-supported public school system, but it made no mention of segregated schools.[6] The following year, the Assembly provided for public schools separated by race. Before schools could be built or otherwise acquired, private schools, already functioning and segregated, were taken over by the state and made a part of the public school system.[7]

Support of the public schools, of course, fell to those who owned taxable property. Thus, the whites bore the major part of the cost of Negro schools in addition to the cost of their own—a burden which at first they seemed not unwilling to assume. In his first annual report, Superintendent of Public Instruction, William H. Ruffner, explained that where there were no public funds for schools, the white people contributed money for white schools and often contributed to the establishment of a proportionate share of Negro schools as well.[8] In 1872, Ruffner observed that, "Our intelligent citizens are becoming more and more favorable to the education of the negro."[9] The next year he reported that, "There is no prevailing disposition among the whites to oppress or cast out the negroes, or to deny to them education."[10] Writing in 1873–1874, Edward King observed that, "The Richmond schools for both white and colored pupils rank among the best in the country. . . . No one thinks of refusing to aid the negro in obtaining his education, although he contributes little or nothing toward the school tax."[11]

General Armstrong of Hampton Institute wrote in 1879: "Our relations with the State of Virginia, as trustee of that part of the land fund devoted to the colored people, have been in all ways satisfactory. Interest has been promptly paid. Throughout the State the

[5] Writers Project of the WPA, *Negro in Virginia*, 270.
[6] *Virginia Constitution of 1869*, Article VIII, Sections 1 and 2.
[7] Taylor, "Negro in the Reconstruction of Virginia," *Journal of Negro History*, XI (1926), 389.
[8] "School Report, 1871," *Annual Reports, 1870–1871*, p. 15.
[9] *Ibid., 1871–1872*, p. 3.
[10] *Ibid., 1872–1873*, p. 203.
[11] King, *Great South*, 638.

feeling is kindly and encouraging to good work for the negro race."[12] W. P. Warren of the New Hampshire State Normal School, attending a meeting of colored teachers at Hampton Institute, in 1881, said of them: "We found them loyal to their State, proud of its history and heartily interested in its advancement; they spoke warmly of the interest taken in the colored schools by the whites, and especially by the local school Superintendents."[13] When Robert R. Moton, while still a student at Hampton Institute, wanted to establish an industrial school of the Hampton type in Cumberland county, he received offers of support from some of the county's leading white people. One offered ten acres of land. The county school superintendent told him that the county would cooperate and would probably pay the teacher's salary.[14]

On the other hand, some whites opposed Negro education from the beginning and their numbers increased as the century approached its end. In 1871, the commissioner of the new Federal Bureau of Education sent out 3,000 questionnaires to both employers and employees to gather information on their estimate of the value of education to laborers. Replies received indicated unanimous agreement that it was beneficial and useful, except for the Southern planters, of whom the majority opposed any education for the Negro. It is reasonable to assume that some of the planters questioned were Virginians.[15] A prominent Funder, Robert L. Dabney, opposed public education of the Negro on the grounds that "the Negro does not need it to fit him for the right of suffrage, since the Negro will soon be stripped of that 'right.'"[16] By 1880, the previously sanguine William H. Ruffner admitted that many white school officials did not deal justly with the Negroes under them—whether teacher or pupils.[17] And, though white teachers in Negro schools were common, a white preacher in the Methodist church who also taught a Negro school in Bedford county, reportedly lost many of his congregation

---

[12] Stowe, "Education of Freedmen," *North American Review*, CXXIX (July, 1879), 92.

[13] Quoted in "School Report, 1881," *Annual Reports, 1880–1881*, p. 78.

[14] Moton, *Finding A Way Out*, 99–100.

[15] Raymond B. Pinchbeck, *The Virginia Negro Artisan and Tradesman*, Phelps-Stokes Fellowship Paper of the University of Virginia (Richmond, Virginia, 1926), 71.

[16] Quoted in Johnston, "Participation of Negroes in the Government of Virginia . . . 1877 to 1888," *Journal of Negro History*, XIV (July, 1929), 255–256.

[17] Hermione Elizabeth Lloyd, "History of the Public Education of the Negro in Virginia," Unpublished M. A. Thesis (Howard University, 1936), 38.

because he taught Negroes.[18] But, as a rule, white people usually saw nothing wrong with white teachers in Negro schools, since "the white teachers occupied the relation of master and mistress to the negro people." [19]

Still other prominent Virginians opposed public education and hence Negro education. In the words of John W. Daniel, later U. S. Senator, "It were better for the State to burn the schools" than to fail to pay any part of the state debt. Independently wealthy, Governor F. W. M. Holliday, called public schools "a luxury . . . to be paid for like any other luxury, by the people who wish their benefits." [20]

By the beginning of the twentieth century, with the Negro in effect disfranchised and with all social equality barred by both practice and statute, there appeared to be less practical need for educating the Negro for a status he was never to achieve. On the principle of "a little education is a dangerous thing. . . ." one white Virginian pointed out that, "To educate the negro for higher things, and then to close all avenues to him, makes the school-house the stepping stone to the penitentiary." [21] He continued:

> Education elevates the negro, hence renders him less tractable and less willing to fulfill the duties of a subservient class; hence it widens the chasm between ⁺he races, and instead of solving the problem, only hastens the period when the inevitable selection of segregation, subordination, or extermination must be made.[22]

In 1901, the University of Virginia's Professor Richard Heath Dabney opposed the education of the Negro on the grounds that it would only serve to make him the industrial competitor of the white man. Added to race antagonism this would only aggravate conditions between the races. Similarly, the editor of *Outlook* magazine concluded that, "The prime reason for not educating the Negro is that he is capable of receiving an education which will make him a rival of the white man." [23]

On the question of *separate* schools for children there was no stiffening of attitude, for, from the beginning, white Virginians were

[18] Oscar Trent Bonner, "A Survey of Negro Education in Bedford County," Unpublished M. A. Thesis (University of Virginia, 1939), 19.
[19] Quoted in Walton, "Negro in Richmond, 1880–1890" M. A. Thesis (Howard University, 1950), 71, from Richmond *Dispatch*, November 6, 1883.
[20] Quoted in Woodward, *Origins of the New South*, 61.
[21] Thomas, *Virginia Constitutional Convention and its Possibilities*, 19.
[22] *Ibid.*, 20.
[23] Editor, "Two Southern Views," *Outlook*, LXIX (November 30, 1901), 810.

determined to maintain separate public schools or no public schools at all. Opposition to mixed schools does seem to have hardened, however, to include teacher training institutions. In 1871, Superintendent Ruffner reported that, "In many of the counties no objection is manifested on the part of any to having one institute for . . . [the training of] both white and colored teachers. Little trouble is apprehended on this subject." [24] With time this view was to change.

In its original form, the Supplementary Civil Rights Bill of 1875 would have forbidden segregation in the public schools. In Virginia this bill was uniformly resisted. The Richmond *Dispatch* characteristically expressed its willingness to see the public school system done away with altogether rather than have mixed schools. [25]

Sampling public opinion throughout the state, Superintendent Ruffner, in 1874, reported that his county superintendents informed him that, while the whites were willing to accept Negro education at largely white, public expense, they would revolt over mixing of the races within the schools. From Brunswick county came the report: "There is still some opposition to our school system, but this would die out if the agitation of the civil rights question could be hushed up." From Campbell county: "The impending 'Civil Rights Bill' has somewhat checked progress." From Elizabeth City and Warwick counties:

> It is . . . the general desire of the colored population to have their schools remain . . . separate from the white schools; and it is . . . the universal determination of all the whites that the operation of the public school system shall come to an end in these counties as soon as the civil rights bill [in its original form] shall become a law.

From Franklin county:

> [If] there should be no Federal interference with our school affairs, the time will soon come when all opposition to public education will have vanished from the county. But should the civil rights bill, or any bill providing for mixed schools be passed by Congress, the white people of this county will, with one voice say, "Away, away with the public school system." [26]

The reaction of other counties was in the same vein. [27]

---

[24] "School Report, 1871," *Annual Reports, 1870–1871*, p. 155.
[25] Richmond *Daily Dispatch*, April 26, 1872.
[26] Quoted in Brown, *Education and Economic Development of the Negro in Virginia*, 51–52 from "School Report, 1874."
[27] *Ibid.*, 52–53.

Superintendent Ruffner declared that,

> . . . it must generally be known that the admixture of whites and
> blacks in southern schools is simply *impossible.* The most obvious
> reason for this is the social disparity, indeed the intense social repug-
> nance, existing between the races . . . we have one of the most ag-
> gravated cases known to history of social repugnance between two
> peoples inhabiting the same territory.[28]

Writing for *Scribners' Monthly*, in opposition to the proposed civil
rights bill, Ruffner maintained that,

> . . . there is a moral reason which . . . prevents coeducation every-
> where that negroes are numerous. They move on a far lower plane
> than the whites, as a class . . . it is enough to say that the average
> character and habits of these people render it highly proper in the
> whites to refuse to associate their children with them in the intimate
> relations of a school.[29]

Advocating separate but equal educational opportunities for Negroes, Ruffner declared: "At least during the present generation
the attempt to mix the white and colored races in the schools of
fifteen States of this Union, is not only . . . impossible . . . but, if
forcibly pressed . . . [will] defeat the general education of both
races."[30] William H. Dixon, an English visitor to the United States,
said of the Virginia public schools in 1875: "Teachers assure you
they could not mix the classes if they tried."[31]

Nor did the Readjusters, usually friendly to public education,
differ on the issue of separate public schools. In 1882, the Readjuster
legislature replaced Ruffner with R. R. Farr as Superintendent of
Public Instruction. On the question of mixed schools, Farr maintained:

> There is no danger of the white and colored schools ever being mixed;
> that is beyond the bounds of probability, is antagonistic to the wishes
> of both races, and would result in the annihilation of public schools at
> least. We [the Readjusters] are so much opposed to it that white
> teachers for [Negro] public schools is too much mixing for us.[32]

---

[28] "School Report, 1874," *Annual Reports, 1873–1874*, pp. 146–147.
[29] William H. Ruffner, "The Co-Education of the White and Colored Races,"
Scribners' Monthly, VIII (1874), 88.
[30] *Ibid.*, 90.
[31] William H. Dixon, *White Conquest* (London, 1876), II, p. 170.
[32] "School Report, 1882," *Annual Reports, 1881–1882*, pp. 64–65. The Readjusters did reduce the number of whites teaching in Negro schools and replaced

In spite of this seeming unanimity, a visitor from the North made some surprising and somewhat prophetic statements in 1882. After observing the separate school systems of the South, J. B. Harrison, who was no Negrophile and who expressed grave doubts as to the Negro's intellectual capacity to develop under even the most favorable circumstances, concluded that, although the Southern whites were "strongly and almost universally opposed to the idea of educating white and black children . . . in the same schools," their position of adamancy was changing. "After attentively studying the subject everywhere [*sic*] I am convinced that there will soon be mixed schools . . . in many parts of the South. There are already a few such schools. . . ." Many of the foremost "Bourbons," he claimed, anticipated that "mixed schools are 'sure to come,' and they are not disturbed by the prospect." One Southern educator told him: "Mixed schools will come, but slowly, and will commence in country places, where there are few colored children. In the cities the higher [*sic*] schools will first mix. The change cannot come suddenly, and it is not desirable that it should." Harrison expected a decided revolution in Southern thought within twenty years.[33]

Five years later, however, the liberal Richmond *Whig* strongly expressed its opposition to any idea of mixed schools, maintaining that the white people would never tolerate them and would abolish the public schools first. The same issue of the *Whig* carried a news notice that the Richmond Democratic Committee had called for the resignation of one of its members, who had dared advocate mixed schools. The member was none other than Lewis H. Blair.[34] Twenty years later, in 1902, contrary to Harrison's forecast, the Virginia Negro had apparently lost all hope of even equal educational opportunity.

While separate schools were objectionable enough to informed Negroes, even more distasteful was the white habit of not giving

them with Negro teachers in some areas, but it is doubtful if they did it out of objection to "too much mixing." Rather they were probably prompted to do this by desire for the Negro vote or by a genuine sense of fair play, for they also created the first mixed school board in Richmond.—Walton, "Negro in Richmond, 1880–1890," M. A. Thesis (Howard University, 1950), 70–71.

[33] Harrison, "Studies in the South," *Atlantic Monthly,* L (1882), 359–360. Harrison's remarks were, however, a generalization for the entire South, in which he did not name names and places. Still, this fact does not rob his observations of merit.

[34] Richmond *Weekly Whig,* July 29, 1887.

Negro teachers jobs in Negro schools if there were white teachers to take them. In the early years of the public school system it was often necessary to staff Negro schools with white teachers—the only ones available. But as time went on and the practice was continued in the face of a growing number of Negro teachers turned out by the St. Stephens Normal School, Richmond Institute, the Hampton Institute, and after 1883, the Virginia Normal and Collegiate Institute, the Negroes began to grow restive. In 1880, the Negroes of Richmond petitioned the city school board to hire all Negro teachers for the Richmond Negro schools, instead of using them in only one of the four groups of Negro schools in the city. They produced statistical evidence to show that both scholarship and attendance were higher in Negro schools taught by Negroes than in Negro schools taught by whites. The petition was denied, in spite of the fact that State Superintendent Ruffner himself maintained that "people are best taught by members of their own race." [35]

Without doubt much of this discrimination against Negro teachers had more of an economic basis than a purely racial one. When white teachers were available and needed jobs, white superintendents employed them in preference to Negro teachers. In 1880, of the 1,256 Negro schools in the state, only 785 had Negro teachers. [36] Still, the fact could not have been lost upon the superintendents that white teachers were not likely to indoctrinate their Negro charges with the philosophy of human equality, while assuredly many Negro teachers would. And white teachers in Negro schools were often accused of lacking sympathy for the Negro. [37]

County superintendencies were, of course, reserved for whites. School boards were also reserved for white membership only. And when, in 1883, the State Board of Education, headed by Readjuster Governor Cameron, discovered a technicality which permitted it to dismiss the Richmond city school board and itself appoint a new one consisting of two Negro members, a storm of white protest arose. Some whites challenged the State Board's peremptory action in removing one board and appointing another, but the courts denied the complaint, and for at least a year the city had to put up with a school

[35] Taylor, "Negro in the Reconstruction of Virginia," *Journal of Negro History*, XI (1926), 402–403.

[36] Writers Project of the WPA, *Negro in Virginia*, 270.

[37] Lloyd, "History of the Public Education of the Negro in Virginia," M. A. Thesis (Howard University, 1936), 35.

board on which there were two Negroes. This board removed twenty-seven white teachers from Negro schools and replaced them with Negro teachers, but, in 1884, conservative forces got their revenge. With defeat of the Readjusters in November, 1883, conservative Democrats at once removed the Negro board members.[38]

The separate schools were never equal. Glaring inequalities existed in the proportionate number of schools provided for the two races, in funds appropriated for operation of Negro schools, and in the salaries of Negro teachers. In the years 1871–1880, when the ratio of whites to Negroes in the state population was three to two, or about sixty to forty percent, the school-building ratio was approximately three to one.[39] In 1871, when there were 2,278 white schools and only 769 schools for Negroes, Dr. Ruffner explained that it was impossible to get qualified teachers of either race for Negro schools.[40] In 1880, there were only 1,256 Negro schools to 3,598 for whites. And, in nine years the number of Negro teachers had increased from 504 in 1871 to only 785 in 1880.[41]

In 1872, Dr. Ruffner admitted that the Negro was not getting his share of public schools but denied that it was intentional. To blame, he said, were (1) frequent unavailability of sufficient funds to provide schools for either race in certain communities, (2) scarcity of suitable teachers for Negro schools, and (3) the fact that many private schools had been given over to the state for use by white children.[42]

In 1874, Miss C. F. Putnam, white teacher of a Negro school in Northumberland county, charged in *The Nation* that, "While the State professes to provide schools (separate schools) for black and white children alike, our observation proves that it is not done." She claimed that Heathsville, the county seat, with nearly equal numbers of white and Negro children and with an appropriation of $500, had spent $450 on white schools and $50 on Negro schools. "The colored schools are not heartily supported, and are purposely of as little

---

[38] Walton, "Negro in Richmond, 1880–1890," M. A. Thesis (Howard University, 1950), 70–71; Pearson, *Readjuster Movement in Virginia*, 163; Eckenrode, "History of Virginia Since 1865," p. 173.

[39] "School Report, 1880," *Annual Reports, 1879–1880*, p. 126.

[40] "School Report, 1871," *Annual Reports, 1870–1871*, p. 15.

[41] "School Report, 1880," *Annual Reports, 1879–1880*, p. 126.

[42] "School Report, 1872," *Annual Reports, 1871–1872*, p. 23.

benefit as possible." [43] Replying to Miss Putnam through the same publication, Ruffner said,

I wrote to the superintendent of schools for that county . . . sending him a copy of your paper, and instructing him to hold a court of investigation, after duly inviting Miss Putnam to be present. . . .

The court was promptly held, and Miss Putnam appeared; but as she was not prepared with evidence, the court was adjourned to a future day.[44]

That Miss Putnam did not produce evidence is not sufficient to discredit her charge, for the evidence which the "court" wanted was undoubtedly held by the school authorities, presuming they kept such financial records.

By 1878, the financial burden of the public schools, plus that of the Funding Act of 1871 providing for the complete payment of pre-war state debt and interest of forty-six million dollars, had become more than the financial resources of the state could bear. Because of "Virginia's unspotted honor," the Funder or debt-paying element demanded that the debt be paid in full and that state services be curtailed as necessary to assure payment. The public schools were one of the first services to be cut back; school funds were dipped into for other purposes at both the state and local levels.[45] The number of white and Negro schools, in 1877, was 3,442 and 1,230 respectively; in 1878, it was reduced to 3,399 and 1,146. But, in 1879, the year which saw the Readjusters swept into power, the number had fallen to 1,816 and 675 respectively.[46]

Without doubt, Funder closing of the schools was a major factor in bringing the Readjusters to office. Immediately, the next year, 1880, the number of schools jumped to 3,598 and 1,256, the highest number up to that time.[47] Still, in that year the white population constituting three-fifths of the total received three-fourths of the school funds.[48] In 1882, R. R. Farr, new State Superintendent of Public

---

[43] *The Nation*, XIX (November 12, 1874), 316.
[44] *Ibid.*, XIX (December 24, 1874), 421.
[45] "School Report, 1879," *Annual Reports, 1878–1879*, p. 4. On the debt question see Pearson, *Readjuster Movement in Virginia;* Massey, *Autobiography of John E. Massey;* Richard L. Morton, *History of Virginia—Virginia Since 1861* (Chicago and New York, 1924). Summary of the debt question above, pp. 16–17.
[46] "School Report, 1880," *Annual Reports, 1879–1880*, p. 126.
[47] *Ibid.*
[48] Pearson, *Readjuster Movement in Virginia*, 61.

Instruction, admitted that the whites had one school for every 77 children of school age, while the Negroes had one school for every 158 children.[49]

Little could be done for the state's financial plight till readjustment of the debt was provided for. Funder Governor F. W. M. Holliday vetoed the Riddleberger Bill, which would have scaled down the debt, and not till 1882, under Readjuster Governor Cameron, did this bill become law. In the same year, $400,000 from the sale of the state's interest in the Atlantic, Mississippi, and Ohio Railroad was designated for use by the public schools. This appropriation put the public school system on a firm footing for the first time.[50]

The Readjuster legislature also provided for the first time a state institution of higher learning open to Negroes of Virginia. Most of the colored teachers had been supplied by the privately endowed Hampton Institute. In 1882, establishment of the Virginia Normal and Collegiate Institute at Petersburg was authorized by the legislature, with an initial appropriation of $100,000 and a stipulated $20,000 annual grant. The $100,000 was also to be paid from proceeds of the sale of the state's interest in the A. M. & O. Railroad. However, a group of die-hard Funders sought an injunction against use of the money for a Negro college, maintaining that the money in question should go into the sinking fund. Fortunately for the cause of education, the courts upheld the legality of the appropriation, and, in 1883, the institution now known as Virginia State College opened its doors to Negro students.[51] With the defeat of the Readjusters in 1883, the annual appropriation was soon reduced from $20,000 to $15,000.[52] And, in March, 1902, the annual appropriation was restricted to "such funds as might seem available to carry on the work." At the same time, the word "Collegiate" was dropped from the name Virginia Normal and Collegiate Institute and the word "Industrial" substituted.[53]

Under the Readjusters, educational inequalities had been alleviated though not removed. The entire public school system had

[49] Brown, *Education and Economic Development of the Negro in Virginia,* 54.
[50] Lloyd, "History of the Public Education of the Negro in Virginia," M. A. Thesis (Howard University, 1936), 36.
[51] "School Report, 1882," *Annual Reports, 1881–1882,* p. 64; Taylor "Negro in the Reconstruction of Virginia," *Journal of Negro History,* XI (1926), 398.
[52] Taylor, "Negro in the Reconstruction of Virginia," *Journal of Negro History,* XI (1926), 414.
[53] Writers Project of the WPA, *Negro in Virginia,* 268.

been put on a firm financial basis and given additional and liberal financial support. And a start was made toward providing higher education for Negroes.[54] Readjuster rule lasted only four years, however, and while the Conservatives, who returned to power in 1884, did not tear down the educational edifice which had been built largely by the Readjusters, they did little to maintain it and less toward adding to it. The 1890's were an economically depressed period generally, and they marked a public school famine. The office of Superintendent of Public Instruction became a mere sinecure. From 1890 to 1898, it was held by the onetime Readjuster, John E. Massey, by then a pronounced foe of Negro education.[55]

Before the Readjusters came to power, the highest proportion of the school-age population ever to be enrolled in the public schools was one-half of the whites, in 1878,[56] and slightly under a third of the Negroes, in 1877.[57] In 1879, the lowest year, only one-fourth of the school-age whites and one-fifth of the Negroes were enrolled.[58] Under the Readjuster regime, Superintendent Ruffner reported that in 1881 enrollment once more reached the peak of the years 1877–1878, with slightly more than half the school-age whites and almost a third of the Negroes enrolled.[59] The last year of the Readjuster era the respective percentages were 56.3 and 37.7.[60]

With return to power of the more conservative Democratic party in 1884, school enrollment did not decline as one might expect. Neither did it rapidly increase, as it had under the Readjusters. Rather there followed only consolidation of the tremendous impetus given the cause of public education by the Readjusters. In 1884, the percentage of white enrollment scarcely changed at all, declining only three-tenths of one percent to 56 percent. For the last time in the century Negro enrollment made a significant increase, from 37.7 to 43 percent.[61] The effects of Readjuster zeal and Negro hopes were still very evident. In 1885, white enrollment jumped to 62 per-

[54] Blake, *William Mahone*, 194–195, 219.
[55] Louis R. Harlan, *Separate and Unequal: Public School Campaigns and Racism in the Southern Seaboard States 1901–1915* (Chapel Hill, N. C., 1958), 135–136.
[56] "School Report, 1878," *Annual Reports, 1877–1878*, p. 2.
[57] *Ibid.*, 1877, *Annual Reports, 1876–1877*, p. 6.
[58] *Ibid.*, 1879, *Annual Reports, 1878–1879*, p. 2.
[59] *Ibid.*, 1881, *Annual Reports, 1880–1881*, p. 68.
[60] *Ibid.*, 1883, *Annual Reports, 1882–1883*, p. 72.
[61] *Ibid.*, 1884, *Annual Reports, 1883–1884*, p. 11.

cent and Negro enrollment climbed to 45 percent.[62] Thereafter, enrollment percentages for both races remained practically static for the rest of the century.[63] In 1899, white enrollment was still only 61 percent and Negro enrollment only 44 percent.[64] There are no figures for 1900.

As they had done in the case of the debt settlement, the Democrats seemed willing to accept Readjuster school reform, which had been demanded by the people. Both were too popular to be undone. Readjuster school progress was accepted because it was good politics to accept it, but there was no continued reform. Not until early in the twentieth century was any signal progress in public education again made. And then it was made in response to renewed popular demand. Already the conservative, political leadership of Virginia's twentieth century Democratic party was revealing the streak of liberal elasticity which would preclude another era of anything like Readjusterism.

By 1900, few white Virginians were any longer advocating education for the Negro to make him as useful a citizen as possible. Now, the typical attitude was that of the Southside's Walter A. Watson, who was horrified at the thought of Negro schoolhouses "turning out your voters by the thousands to meet you, and to meet me at the ballot box."[65]

In spite of poor support of the public schools, especially Negro schools, and of salary differentials between white and Negro teachers,[66] the percentage of Negro illiteracy steadily decreased from an estimated 86 percent in 1870, to 74 percent in 1880, 57 percent in 1890, and 45 percent in 1900.[67]

In education as in other areas, Lewis H. Blair was the practical conscience of Virginia and the South, reiterating again and again what to him was simple logic: relegation of the Negro to an inferior status by discrimination and segregation dragged down the level of

[62] *Ibid.*, 1885, *Annual Reports, 1884–1885*, p. 13.
[63] The respective enrollment percentages for white and colored were: 1886, 58 and 44; 1887, 59 and 45; 1888, 61 and 45; 1889, 64 and 46; 1890, 63 and 45; 1891, 58 and 45; 1892, 56 and 42; 1893, 60 and 44; 1894, 61 and 44; 1895, 59 and 45; 1896, 6. 5 and 45; 1897, 61.5 and 46; 1898, 63 and 47; and 1899, 61 and 44—"School Reports" for those years in *Annual Reports*.
[64] "School Report, 1899," *Annual Reports, 1898–1899*, p. XIV.
[65] Quoted in Harlan, *Separate and Unequal*, 136.
[66] Martin, "Negro Disfranchisement in Virginia," *Howard University Studies in the Social Sciences*, I, p. 94.
[67] Lloyd, "History of Public Education of the Negro in Virginia," M. A. Thesis (Howard University, 1936), 33, 42; U. S. *Census Report*, 1900.

achievement in all areas of the *whole* South. Advocating an end to separate schools for the good of all, Blair prophetically declared:

> The remedy . . . [for raising the educational level of the South] is a radical and far reaching one, and is no less than the abandonment of the principle of separate schools, which principle is an efficient and certain mode of dooming to perpetual ignorance both whites and blacks in thinly-settled areas.[68]
> . . . the whites must through this system [of separate schools] be very great, if not the greatest sufferers, because they have most to lose.[69]

On the inherent inequality of separate schools, Blair anticipated the Supreme Court by sixty-five years when he maintained that,

> Separate schools are a public proclamation to all of African or mixed blood that they are an inferior caste. . . . Hence it follows that separate schools brand the stigma of degradation upon one-half of the population . . . and crushes [*sic*] their hope and and self respect, without which they can never become useful and valuable citizens.[70]
> Separate schools poison at its very source the stream whence spring the noblest fruits of education.[71]

That the South could lay few claims to intellectual and cultural achievements, and that there was even less common appreciation for the products of human thought and reason,[72] Blair found not at all surprising.

> When children are taught, as separate schools practically do, that superiority consists in a white skin, they will naturally be satisfied with that kind of superiority, and they will not willingly undergo the tedious, painful, and patient ordeal requisite to prepare them for superiority in science, art, literature. . . .[73]

[68] Blair, *Prosperity of the South Dependent Upon the Elevation of the Negro*, 98.
[69] *Ibid.*, 101.
[70] *Ibid.*, 99.
[71] *Ibid.*, 108.
[72] In 1880, there were published in the South 128 daily papers with a circulation of 196,533, and 1,612 other publications (weekly papers, magazines, etc.) with a circulation of 1,504,424. In the same year, there were published in all the other states 843 daily papers with a circulation of 3,369,862, and 9,702 other publications with a circulation of 26,708,867. By 1887, the number of Southern daily papers had increased to only 156, while that of the other states reached 1,155. Other publications that year were 1,783 and 10,988 respectively.—Blair, *Prosperity of the South Dependent Upon the Elevation of the Negro*, 89.
[73] *Ibid.*, 109–110.

Thus, in education as in politics, transportation, and other public services, a distinct regression had taken place by 1900 in white attitudes and practices in according to the Negro his rights of manhood and citizenship. Where once there had been at least *some* acceptance of the idea that with time the Negro would gradually become a full-fledged citizen, by 1900 there was almost universal white agreement that he must remain forever a race apart. And neither education nor time, the whites believed, could lift the Negro from his inferior status. And finally, since he was to remain an inferior, there was little reason for educating him for a future he would never know.

Chapter 9

The Crimes of Lynching and Rape and Discrimination in the Adminisration of Justice

THE Virginia Negro found that he was also a second-class citizen before the bar of justice. He was often the victim of harsher punishment than was meted out to whites, and often it was dispensed by Judge Lynch. He was made to do prison labor assigned to Negroes only, where his death-rate was higher than that of whites. Even though he might be a good citizen and perhaps educated, he stood little chance of serving on either a grand or *petit* jury even when the offender was a Negro. On the other hand, he had a much higher crime rate than that of the general population. Because of this high crime rate and because whites believed he was peculiarly addicted to rape, whites often resorted to lynching as punishment for this crime. In reality, however, it cannot be proved that a high incidence of lynching corresponded with a high incidence of rape.

There is considerable evidence revealing the Negro's position before the bar of justice. In 1872, Miss Elizabeth Van Lew of Richmond, charged that there were in the state penitentiary upwards of 200 Negroes who were guilty of "no other crime than that of being Republicans." [1] That same year, the white superintendent of a Petersburg tobacco factory whipped a Negro boy for neglecting his work; the superintendent was arrested but the judge dismissed the case. [2] A. S. Pryor, principal of the Negro schools in Petersburg, charged in 1882 that, "We [Negroes] have . . . been arraigned before packed tribunals on pseudo charges and have been the recipient of unjust stripes and scars." [3] ("Unjust stripes and scars" referred to the whipping post, abolished that same year by the Readjusters.)

The Negro's high crime-rate, itself a product of his depressed status, was made a two-edged sword against him in 1876, when

---

[1] Taylor, "Negro in the Reconstruction of Virginia," *Journal of Negro History*, XI (1926), 326, as cited from the Richmond *Daily Dispatch*, January 5, 1872.
[2] *Ibid.*, 324, as cited from the Richmond *Daily Dispatch*, June 8, 1872.
[3] Richmond *Weekly Whig*, September 15, 1882.

135

petty larceny was added to the list of more serious crimes leading to disfranchisement.[4] Some idea of the effectiveness of this measure can be gained from the fact that, in the hustings court of the city of Richmond alone, approximately 1,000 Negroes were disfranchised between 1870 and 1892 when convicted of felony or petty larceny.[5] Meanwhile, another thousand Negroes were disfranchised in the police court of the same city between 1877 and 1892 for conviction of petty larceny alone.[6] In all likelihood, the proportions of Negro disfranchisement were equally high for Petersburg, Norfolk, Danville, and rural areas with large Negro populations.

Discrimination inside the prisons and jails was even more flagrant. Here the truth rarely leaked out, and there was absolutely no chance to correct the malpractices. Worse still was the convict lease system, whereby the state leased convict labor to private industry such as quarries, mines, fertilizer plants, and canal and railroad building companies. One Southern historian declared that in the last quarter of the nineteenth century, the convict lease system "left a trail of dishonor and death that could find a parallel only in the persecutions of the Middle Ages or in the prison camps of Nazi Germany." [7] Outside of the South, only the states of Nebraska and Washington and the territory of New Mexico still utilized the convict lease system.[8]

Because of Negroes' higher crime rate, but also because of the tendency to show little leniency toward Negro offenders,[9] the number of Negroes annually admitted to the state penitentiary greatly exceeded the number of whites admitted. For instance, during the years 1871–1878, an annual average of 67 whites and 247 Negroes were imprisoned.[10] Although the tendency was to lease the Negroes to private industries as work battalions, rarely were white men so

---

[4] *Appletons' Annual Cyclopaedia* (1876), 800.

[5] "Official List of Colored Persons Convicted of Felony or Petit Larceny in the Hustings Court of the City of Richmond, and thereby Disfranchised," *Official Lists of Dead, Lunatic, and Convicted Colored Males who are thereby Disfranchised* (Richmond, Virginia, October 24, 1892), n.p. Pamphlet in McGregor Collection of the University of Virginia Library.

[6] "Official List of Colored Persons Convicted of Petit Larceny in the Police Court of the City of Richmond, and thereby Disfranchised," *Official Lists of . . . Colored Males . . . Disfranchised*, n.p.

[7] Fletcher M. Green, "Some Aspects of the Convict Lease System in the Southern States," *Essays in Southern History: The James Sprunt Studies in History and Political Science*, XXXI (1949), 122.

[8] *Ibid.*, 119.

[9] Taylor, "Negro in the Reconstruction of Virginia," *Journal of Negro History*, XI (1926), 292.

[10] Morton, *Negro in Virginia Politics*, 135–136.

leased. Usually only 3 or 4 whites were leased out in a year, although in 1871, the number reached 53.[11] In 1877, when there were 561 Negro prisoners serving as leased labor, not a single white man was so leased. At the same time, there were 235 white men and 6 white women in the penitentiary, along with 316 Negro men and 94 Negro women.[12] Most of the leased Negroes were turned over either to railroads or to the Old Dominion Granite Company. After 1880, the firm leasing them was no longer named, the official reports reading only, "leased to the public works."

    The harshest of working and living conditions seem to have existed on the James River and Kanawha Canal project, where large numbers of prisoners were leased in 1878 and 1879—349 Negroes and 37 whites in 1878,[13] and 207 Negroes and 15 whites in 1879.[14] In 1878, 32 of those prisoners died, or over 8 percent of the total employed there, as a result of cold, wet working conditions and admitted ill treatment and care.[15] In 1879, the death-rate declined to about 5 percent, but it was still twice the death-rate in the penitentiary. This time, however, it was claimed that the high death-rate was due only to the harsh working conditions and not to ill treatment or physical neglect.[16]

    Negro deaths, whether in the penitentiary or on lease outside, were always proportionally much higher than the Negro percentage of total prisoners. For example, in 1878, 48 Negro and 2 white prisoners died; in 1879, 27 Negroes and 2 whites; in 1881, 36 Negroes and 3 whites; in 1882, 30 Negroes and 3 whites. The Readjusters apparently did little if anything to improve conditions of Negro prisoners. In 1878 and 1879, most of the deaths resulted from dysentery, diarrhea, pneumonia, and tuberculosis—the products of poor food, shelter, and sanitation and harsh working conditions. In 1881, most of the deaths were due to accidents and diarrhea; in 1882, to pneumonia, diarrhea, and tuberculosis, contracted on the "public works." [17]

    Within the penitentiary as well, the death-rate remained dispro-

---

[11] Taylor, "Negro in the Reconstruction of Virginia," *Journal of Negro History*, XI (1926), 291-292.

[12] "Report of the Board of Directors of the State Penitentiary, 1877," *Annual Reports, 1876–1877*, p. 17.

[13] *Ibid.*, 1878, *Annual Reports, 1877–1878*, p. 25.

[14] *Ibid.*, 1879, *Annual Reports, 1878–1879*, p. 23.

[15] *Ibid.*, 1878, *Annual Reports, 1877–1878*, p. 42.

[16] *Ibid.*, 1879, *Annual Reports, 1878–1879*, pp. 6, 37.

[17] *Ibid.*, 1878, pp. 42–43; 1879, p. 40; 1881, pp. 52–53; 1882, p. 38, *Annual Reports, 1877–1878, 1878–1879, 1880–1881, 1881–1882*.

portionately high for Negroes. In 1872, 24 Negroes died there, mostly from pneumonia and tuberculosis, as contrasted with only 1 white prisoner, aged 74; in 1874, 18 Negroes and 2 whites, mostly from pneumonia and typhoid fever; in 1876, 10 Negroes and 3 whites; and in 1877, 21 Negroes and 6 whites died, mostly of tuberculosis.[18] Throughout the remainder of the century, the situation remained essentially the same.[19]

Of penitentiary conditions, the board of directors itself admitted, in 1875:

> On a recent thorough examination of the [state penitentiary] building by the directors, not unfrequently four or five . . . convicts were confined in a small room, badly ventilated and imperfectly warmed— a state of things which must engender disease, as well as endanger the security of the inmates.[20]

That the directors' assessment was correct, the death statistics cited above afford ample proof.

Discrimination in the administration of justice was particularly to be seen in the matter of jury duty. Campbell found the Negro in Virginia systematically excluded from jury duty in the state courts. The whites, he said, excused this by saying, "They have got votes, and we cannot give them everything." On the other hand, Campbell claimed that Negroes did serve on juries in Federal courts located in Virginia.[21]

In 1900, George Thomas Stephenson sent letters to the court clerks of every county in the South in which Negroes made up one-half or more of the population, requesting information on the use of Negroes on juries, the reaction to their use, and the increasing or decreasing frequency of their use. He received replies from eleven Virginia counties. Nine counties claimed to have used Negro jurors at one time or another, but of this number seven counties reported that the practice had markedly decreased since about 1885. Generally, the replies indicated that Negro jurors' service was not highly esteemed or even widely accepted. Only one county reported regular use of

---

[18] *Ibid.*, 1872, p. 21; 1874, p. 22; 1876, p. 34; 1877, p. 34, *Annual Reports, 1871–1872, 1873–1874, 1875–1876, 1876–1877.*
[19] *Ibid.*, *Annual Reports* (1880–1900).
[20] *Ibid.*, 1875, *Annual Reports, 1874–1875*, p. 3.
[21] Campbell, *White and Black*, 291.

Negro jurors; this county also commented favorably upon their services.[22] Unfortunately, none of the counties was named.

George M. Arnold, a Lynchburg Negro, claimed in 1879 that as a result of Conservative party control of the state and the election of Conservative judges who appointed the juries, not three Negroes in the entire state had been appointed to serve on *petit* juries since the end of Governor Gilbert C. Walker's administration in January, 1874. Arnold continued:

> . . . also on recent juries I *have seen this with my own eyes* [white] men were on the jury to try cases wherein colored men were to be tried, who from one day the beginning of the year, to the last day the ending of it, have no visible means of support and are known as "men of the town."

Meanwhile, Arnold said, in the cities of Norfolk, Richmond, Petersburg, and Lynchburg, there were large communities of intelligent Negro businessmen who were regularly excluded from jury duty.[23]

There were, however, interesting exceptions to the practice of jury exclusion. On March 29, 1871, Judge James Kenny of Harrisonburg wrote in his diary: "The Grand Jury is made up of whites and negroes, & the novelty of negroes in the Jury box has attracted all the idle & curious persons to the Court House."[24] Again, in 1880, in Harrisonburg, a Negro by the name of James Cochran was a member of the grand jury.[25] In both cases this was probably a Federal grand jury, since Harrisonburg was the seat of the United States Court for the Western District of Virginia, and since Negroes did sometimes serve on juries in the Federal courts of Virginia.[26] On December 1, 1879, the first all-Negro jury was empaneled in Albemarle county at Charlottesville. They sat in judgment of a Negro man charged with shooting with intent to kill. An all-white jury had earlier failed to reach a verdict. The Negro jury found him guilty and he was sentenced to sixty days in the county jail. One reporter of the trial commented on the apparent intelligence of the jury and claimed that

---

[22] George Thomas Stephenson, *Race Distinctions in American Law* (New York, 1910), 253, 269–271.
[23] George M. Arnold to Isaiah H. Wears, November 20, 1879, Aptheker, ed., *Documentary History of the Negro People in U. S.*, 728–729.
[24] Quoted in John W. Wayland, *Historic Harrisonburg* (Staunton, Va., 1949), 41.
[25] Wayland, *History of Rockingham County*, 240.
[26] Campbell, *White and Black*, 291.

140   *Race Relations in Virginia, 1870–1902*

the novelty of a colored jury attracted a large crowd.[27] In Martins-
ville, in 1882, a Negro was tried before a mixed jury of seven whites
and five Negroes for the killing of a white man.[28]

Attempts were made by the Federal courts in Virginia to prevent
the systematic exclusion of Negroes from jury duty in the state courts,
and to assure the presence of some Negro members on all juries
trying Negro defendants. This was done on the grounds that deliber-
ate exclusion of Negroes from jury duty was an open violation of the
Fourteenth Amendment, and in the belief that it was doubtful
whether the Negroes enjoyed equal protection of the laws before an
all-white jury. These attempts availed little.

In 1878, a Judge Coles of a county court was indicted in the
Federal Court for the Western District of Virginia for excluding
Negroes from the jury lists because of their race. Both Judge Coles
and the state of Virginia brought before the Supreme Court a
petition for a *writ* of *habeas corpus*, averring that the finding of the
indictment, his arrest, and imprisonment were unconstitutional. The
petition of Judge Coles and the state was denied,[29] but it is not
clear whether the charge was proven.

The following year, 1879, Judge Alexander Rives of the Federal
Court for the Western District of Virginia, instructed a grand jury
to indict several Virginia counties for the offense of not summoning Negroes to jury duty.[30] Earlier that same year, Judge Rives had
removed a convicted Negro from the hands of the state on the
grounds that, having been convicted by an all-white jury, he had not
enjoyed the right of equal protection of the laws conferred upon him
by the Fourteenth Amendment.[31] In 1880, again in Judge Rives'
court, a Judge Hill was acquitted by a jury of ten whites and two
Negroes of charges of not summoning Negroes to jury duty. Argument was not even presented, as the evidence against him completely
broke down.[32]

Various completely unsuccessful legislative attempts were made
to assure the Negro equal chance of selection for jury duty. In 1872,

[27] Covington *Alleghany Tribune*, December 12, 1879.
[28] Richmond *Weekly Whig*, April 21, 1882.
[29] "Ex Parte Virginia," *United States Supreme Court Reports*, edited by Stephen
K. Williams, C, p. 676.
[30] *The Nation*, XXVIII (March 13, 1879), 173.
[31] *Ibid.*, (January 23, 1879), 60.
[32] *Ibid.*, XXX (March 25, 1880), 223.

the House committee for courts of justice had referred to it a motion which would have guaranteed to all Negro defendants trial before juries consisting of one-half Negro membership. The committee reported that "the law at present makes provision for the qualification of jurors, and it is inexpedient to amend it as proposed." The body of the House concurred.[33] In the Senate, in 1873, the committee for courts of justice received a resolution directing it to look into and report on legislation, if any, necessary to prevent exclusion of Negroes from jury duty. The committee reported that such legislation was "unnecessary," as Negroes were not excluded from jury service "by law." The body of the Senate concurred.[34] The next year, the same question was again raised in the Senate, and the committee for courts of justice reported that legislation to prevent exclusion of Negroes from jury service was "inexpedient." The body of the Senate voted to postpone the whole subject indefinitely.[35] In 1879, another attempt was made in the Senate to guarantee to Negroes the right of jury service, when a resolution was referred to the committee for courts of justice *directing* it to report such a bill.[36] There is no record of any action being taken by the committee.

In face of popular indisposition to place Negroes on juries and legislative indisposition to guarantee them this right of jury service, it was wholly misleading and in part false for the *Dispatch* to declare that, "Nobody here objects to serving on juries with negroes. No [white] lawyer objects to practicing law in a court where negro lawyers practice. In a word, the negro is denied no right to which he is entitled as a citizen." [37] In 1880, at a time when there were 125 white lawyers in Richmond, there were but two Negro lawyers in the city. Nine years later, and three years after the *Dispatch's* statement, the proportion was 100 to 4.[38] In spite of the *Dispatch's* reassurance on the Negro's rights, mixed marriages had been legislated against in 1873 and 1878, and declared null and void in 1879.[39] In practice, Negroes could expect service at almost no restaurant or hotel; they were segregated in the theatres and at times on

[33] *Journal of the House of Delegates, 1872–1873*, pp. 78, 124, 137.
[34] *Journal of the Senate, 1872–1873*, pp. 169, 194, 245.
[35] *Ibid.*, 1874, pp. 353, 355–356, 395.
[36] *Ibid.*, 1879–1880, p. 54.
[37] Richmond *Daily Dispatch*, October 13, 1886.
[38] Walton, "Negro in Richmond, 1880–1890," M. A. Thesis (Howard University, 1950), 50.
[39] Writers Project of the WPA, *Negro in Virginia*, 237.

the railroads.⁴⁰ Intimidation was used to keep the Negroes from voting.⁴¹ By the state's own admission they did not receive their share of public school funds.⁴²

It is well known that many more Negroes than whites were lynched during the period under discussion. Although Negroes were lynched for all manner of alleged offenses, including "uppitiness," Southern whites have traditionally believed that most Negroes were lynched because of sexual attacks upon white women. Moreover, Southern whites have apparently believed that the Negro has a peculiar and almost compelling desire to possess white women. Yet the truth was, more often than not, that the offense precipitating the lynching was one other than rape or attempted rape. The facts were further distorted by claims that, as the generation of Negroes born after the Civil War grew to maturity and sought social equality, the incidence of rape of white women markedly increased.⁴³ One historian maintains that, "In the decade of the nineties, contemporary evidence of all kinds shows that the number of rapings by negro men were [*sic*] increasing at an alarming rate." ⁴⁴ The truth is, in Virginia at least, that the incidence of rape did increase between 1870 and 1910, and it increased faster than the increase in population. But no especial case can be made out against the nineties. As many, or more, prisoners were committed to the state penitentiary for rape or attempted rape in 1873, 1875, 1876, and 1877, as there were in 1891, 1894, and 1895.⁴⁵ And as many were lynched for the same crime in 1880 as in 1891, 1892, and 1893,⁴⁶ the last being the peak year of lynchings in Virginia.

However, it must be remembered that the accusation of attempted rape was lightly and carelessly made by white Southerners. A Negro burglar of a place where a white woman was, or a Negro peeping-tom, was perhaps as likely to be charged with attempted rape as with the true offense. Therefore the incidence of attempted rape was

⁴⁰ Taylor, "Negro in the Reconstruction of Virginia," *Journal of Negro History*, XI (1926), 294–296.
⁴¹ Mahone Papers for November 21–30, 1883; Eppes-Kilmartin Papers.
⁴² "School Report, 1872," *Annual Reports, 1871–1872*, p. 23; Brown, *Education and Economic Development of the Negro in Virginia*, 53–54.
⁴³ Thomas Nelson Page, *The Negro: The Southerner's Problem* (New York, 1904), 96; Goode, *Recollections of a Lifetime*, 226–227.
⁴⁴ Morton, *Negro in Virginia Politics*, 136–137.
⁴⁵ "Report[s] of the Superintendent of the State Penitentiary" for those years, in *Annual Reports*.
⁴⁶ *Journal of the Senate, 1897–1898*, p. 47.

not as high as reported. Likewise, lynching statistics are deceiving, because many lynchings were undoubtedly covered up by such explanations as "shot while resisting arrest" or "shot while attempting to escape." By this token the number of lynchings was probably much greater than reported.

In reality few sound conclusions can be drawn from the available statistical evidence on lynchings and rape. This evidence does demonstrate, however, that the increase in lynchings did not by any means correlate with an increase in the crime of rape. These data further suggest that history supports the contention of sociologists, namely that racial aggression both within a minority race and between that race and the majority race is often in proportion to the degree of repression and frustration felt by the minority.[47] And, in the case of Southern history in the last quarter of the nineteenth century, the economic frustration experienced by the majority of Southern whites, who probably proceeded to take it out on the Negro, further explains the high rate of lynching, especially for such years as the economically depressed one of 1893.

For the Virginia Negro there was truly no hiding place and no refuge from the long arm of white supremacy. Even the scales of justice could not be made to balance when Negro rights and equal treatment were concerned. For many, in their bitterness, the Emancipation Proclamation and the Thirteenth Amendment seemed to be hollow victories, while the Fourteenth and Fifteenth Amendments were a mockery.

---

[47] Gordon W. Allport, *The Nature of Prejudice* (Cambridge, Massachusetts, 1954), 349; Gunnar Myrdal, *An American Dilemma: The Negro Problem and Modern Democracy* (New York and London, 1944), vols. 1–2 in one, 763–764.

Conclusion

RACE relations in Virginia markedly deteriorated between 1870 and 1900. This is not to imply that they were ever in this period excellent or good but even such as they were, they steadily deteriorated. The reasons for this process are complicated, and many of them must be considered in explaining the deterioration in race relations throughout the whole South in this period. On the other hand, there are facets to the story which are peculiar to Virginia, again earning for her the appelation of "different" from her sister Southern states.

While the white population of Virginia never openly welcomed Negroes as citizens and voters, in the very early 1870's, at least, there seems to have existed a sportsmanlike, if grudging, acceptance of them, with no great resentment or anger over the fact that they nearly all voted Republican. Later this was not so, and the greater the Democratic majority in the legislature, the more resentment the Negroes met as voters and especially as Republicans.

The cardinal factor in bringing about this hopeful situation was the fact that Virginia passed from Military Reconstruction directly into the hands of white Conservatives. A liberal constitution which they did not like, but which they knew to be not half so bad as they claimed, together with only twenty-seven Negro legislators —twenty-four of them Republicans—could not embitter white Virginians as a Radical-dominated government would have done.

Since the Conservative party was a motley coalition of Liberal Republicans and former Whigs as well as old-line Democrats, it was hardly likely that that party's leadership would be so foolhardy as to make the word "Republican" a term of opprobrium before it was perfectly safe to do so. And it was not believed to be a safe policy before 1873. Until then, the Conservatives often deliberately sought Negro support because it was politically astute to do so. But in the elections of 1873, confident of their majority, they drew the color line.

About the same time, with the advent of a lengthy depression and the exposure of the Grant Administration scandals, the Northern moral pressure to which the South increasingly had been subjected since at least 1831 began to slacken. The North was forced to turn to its own economic problems and to the restoration of some measure of order and morality in its own house. And as Northern pressure upon the South decreased, that region proportionately increased its pressure upon the Negro. Thus, by 1879 the Republican party in Virginia had been reduced to impotence in state affairs, at least. Meanwhile, the Negro had been politically intimidated by disfranchising measures including the poll tax, whipping post, and conviction of petty theft.

Ironically, the four Readjuster years which followed (1880–1883 inclusive) and which resulted in the Negro's gaining even more than he had lost, were also the years which did most to embitter white Virginians against him. There is no evidence that the Virginia Negro did anything to earn this increased and bitter vindictiveness, and there is no more cause for just criticism of the Readjuster regime than there is for criticism of the Conservative one which preceded it or the Democratic one which followed it. For the Readjusters, there is much more to be said in their praise than may be said for either their predecessors or their successors.

The branding of the Readjuster years as years of "Negro rule and ruin," when they were in reality years of more nearly equal justice for the Negro and of constructive progress for the whole state, was the work of the Democratic party politicians and the press they controlled. Coupled with this fact was the tendency of the mass of white Virginians to believe what they were told by a leadership more often than not coming from the traditional ruling class. Most leaders who were not born to that class, excepting Mahone of course, were careful to identify themselves with it and to stand for values dear to that class—rule by the classes and not the masses, identification with the land and training in the law, and the conviction that the Negro race was created to serve them.

In 1883, Readjuster rule ended, primarily because the Readjuster party fell apart from internal dissension, but also because, having fulfilled its mission of scaling down the state debt, revitalizing the public school system, and bringing about other needed reforms, the party had become bankrupt of further ideas and programs of reform. With the Readjuster demise, the Democrats proceeded to cloak that party in obloquy as they consolidated their own hold upon the state and established one-party rule. Their propaganda campaign was so successful that when white Virginians even today speak of the "dark days of Negro rule" in the late last century, they recall the progressive rule of the Readjusters and earlier Military Reconstruction. Virginia never experienced radical-dominated Political Reconstruction of the sort known by her sister states following the end of Military Reconstruction. Thus, a campaign of political propaganda discredited Virginia's most thoroughly democratic and progressive movement since the days of Thomas Jefferson.

The experience with Readjusterism had a marked effect upon Virginia for the rest of the nineteenth century. The Readjuster party brought about reforms which the rest of the South did not know till the rise of Populism. This liberal experience, which the Democrats thoroughly discredited by falsely associating it with Negro rule and by exaggerating Readjuster excesses, stemmed the Populist tide before it reached full bloom in Virginia. A mild brand of Populism was instead guided and directed by respectable Virginians of good family who fell heir to Populist party leadership.

Following the class movement of Readjusterism, the Democratic party and the Democratic press succeeded in convincing white Virginians that the white race, regardless of economic class, must stand together against the Negroes. Economic and social issues had to take second-place to the Negro question. The cry was raised that white men could not divide politically so long as the Negro voted, and a small group of independent Democrats set out to disfranchise the Negro. In the end, Democratic conservatives headed off division of the white vote by rigid machine control of the state and by disfranchisement of the lower class of whites as well as Negroes.

The 1890's saw the cementing of Democratic party control of the electorate, complete removal of the Negro from the state legislature, and disfranchisement of the Negro in practice, though the final stroke had to wait till 1902. Yet at no time in the years after 1870 was there any universal, popular, or general demand that the Negro be disfranchised, as was so often claimed by contemporary political leaders, and has since been repeated by later writers. The power of the Negro vote was at times feared; at all times the Negro voter was likely to be used, bribed, and cheated; but never did the white populace demand his disfranchisement. The best evidence of this is that the people themselves, in 1882, repealed a poll tax amendment which had disfranchised many poor whites and Negroes; in 1888 and in 1897 they rejected proposals that a constitutional convention be held, though admittedly disfranchisement was not overtly made the main reason for holding such a convention; and in 1900, when a constitutional convention was approved with the issue of disfranchisement the clearest reason for calling the convention, the people by their small, apathetic vote showed little interest in the so-called "burning issue." By that date, the Negro had in effect been disfranchised by the Walton Act of 1894 and its amended version of 1896. The Walton Act was the work only of politicians in a Democratically-controlled legislature, not that of the people. The demand for disfranchisement came from a relatively small group of those same Democratic politicians plus a few lily-white Republicans. The sounding board for this demand was a vociferous and Democratically-controlled press.

In the realm of public education, the Negro was early made to know that whatever education he got at public expense must be obtained in segregated schools. Until the very late nineteenth century, there seemed to be no considerable opposition by the whites to a rudimentary public education for the Negro, because it promised to make him a more useful and enlightened citizen. But never were the separate educational facilities equal. By 1879, the cause of public education for both black and white had been severely crippled by the Conservatives as they followed a general policy of reaction and retrenchment. It remained for the Readjusters to put the public school system on a sound footing, which they did between 1879 and 1883. Following Readjuster defeat in the latter year, the resurgent Conservatives (now calling themselves Democrats) made no attempt to undo the educational achievements of the Readjusters, but neither did they continue to improve on them. Educationally, the remainder of the century represented years of stultification. Subsequently, with complete disfranchisement of the Negro, there seemed to be less need for the education of Negroes who could no longer vote.

As a minority group, largely poor and impoverished, and either former slaves or their descendants, the Negro found, not surprisingly, that the scales of justice could not be made to balance where he was concerned. Like all socially and economically depressed groups, the Negro established a crime rate much higher than that of the whites generally, and this fact was used by the politicians and the conservative press to justify keeping him in a position of second-class citizenship. His crime-rate was also greatly exaggerated, particularly with regard to the offense of rape. And the alleged high and increasing incidence of Negroes' raping white women was used to justify actual lynch violence against the Negro. In this setting, the Negro was generally, but not always, excluded from jury duty. As a defendant, he was more likely to be found guilty than a white man. When accused of the same offense as a white man, he was likely to receive a sentence more severe than the white man's. In prison, his lot was almost always made more physically and mentally unbearable than that of the white man. All this tended to breed hopelessness and perpetuate a high Negro crime-rate.

Meanwhile, the Negro had made a small measure of progress in the social realm even as relations on the political scene deteriorated. This created the seeming anomaly of the Negro's gaining socially while he lost politically. But in reality the situation was anomalous only on the surface. Social progress, though severely limited, was determined by the whole people and reflected their attitudes. Political regression was largely the work of both Democratic and Republican party leaders—politicians whose chief aim was to control the vote and who knew that making the Negro the scapegoat of the social ills of the day would appeal to most white voters.

While the Negro was being driven from the polls, he was gaining increasing acceptance of the right to ride the state's railroads in seats of his own choosing. That he did not make commensurate gains in other areas, such as accommodation in hotels, restaurants, and theatres, is at least as much due to the fact that he made no concerted fight for those rights as it is due to any "natural prejudice" by the white man. He won the right to sit where he chose in interstate railroad travel by taking the matter into the Federal courts, and he won increasing acceptance of the right to sit where he chose in intrastate travel by insisting upon the right in great numbers. And never at any time did there develop universal demand that he be relegated to Jim Crow cars. Only a few Democratic newspapers voiced this demand, and there is not sufficient evidence to prove that they spoke for the majority of the people. Meanwhile, the whole issue was obscured by referring to those rights as social rights when they were in reality only civil rights.

All this is not to deny that almost universal prejudice against the Negro did exist. It did. But prejudice did not rule out increasing acceptance, even if that acceptance was granted grudgingly, as it usually was. Neither did prejudice demand disfranchisement nor segregation by statute. Yet it cannot be denied that a highly prejudiced press influenced an already prejudiced white people to accept both as natural, inevitable, and right. As a political issue, the Negro was too tempting for the politicians to let alone. When the issue of the Negro promised to suit their ends, they used it. When a reduced electorate appeared to be advantageous, they disfranchised him. The Virginia legislators who disfranchised the Negro and segregated him by statute *were not* led by representatives of that class of white people who competed directly with the Negro economically and who were more likely to be thrown with him socially. Instead, men of good family and social prestige led the fight.

In the light of all the foregoing evidence, how valid is the Woodward thesis? Were race relations, at least in post-bellum Virginia, much more amicable and amiable than they became after about the mid-1890's? Did the Negro once ride the trains unsegregated and without resort to discrimination? Was it once possible for him, at least occasionally, to enter restaurants, hotels (especially the dining rooms), waiting rooms, bars, theatres, and other public places of amusement without meeting a wall of segregation and ostracism? And finally, did segregation legislation of the late 1890's and early twentieth century create new mores, instead of merely placing a stamp of legal approval upon those already generally existent?

The Woodward thesis is essentially sound. Of course certain qualifications must be made, but they do not destroy or greatly impair its essential validity. The Woodward thesis must also be evaluated in the complete context of *The Strange Career of Jim Crow*, where Professor Woodward himself qualifies it, offers it tentatively and with reserve, and denies all claims of a golden age in Southern race relations in the 1870's and 1880's. The danger is that one is tempted to accept the Woodward thesis at complete face value as the whole answer. It is also easy to deduce or conclude too much, as Professor Woodward sometimes does, from relatively few and isolated occurrences.

This much, however, can be said for it in the case of Virginia: While the Negro was increasingly used, abused, and driven from the

polls by the politicians in the periods, 1873–1878, and 1884–1902—
the interval being the Readjuster era—at no time was it the general demand of the white populace that the Negro be disfranchised
and white supremacy made the law of the land. At the time the railroad segregation statute was passed in 1900, the Negro sat where
he pleased and among white passengers on perhaps a majority of the
state's railroads. Occasionally the Negro met no segregation when
he entered restaurants, bars, waiting rooms, theatres, and other public places of amusement; most of the time, however, he did meet
segregation, opposition, or eviction, and this is the weakest part
of the Woodward thesis. But it must be remembered that the
newspapers and individual authors who commented on the passing
scene were essentially conservative and prone to record a Negro's
being thrown out of a restaurant, for example, rather than his being
served in one. Segregation in these areas does, however, seem to have
been more general in Virginia than in two of the most conservative
Southern states, South Carolina and Mississippi. Detailed studies
have been made of the Negro in these states in this era.[1] There is
much in these two works which tends to support the Woodward
thesis, thus offsetting some negative findings in the case of Virginia.

The real value of the Woodward thesis is that it furnishes
historians with a wholly new and fresh approach to the study of the
racial question in the South for the post-Military Reconstruction
years. It is a milestone in scholarship which cannot be ignored.

---

[1] George Brown Tindall, *South Carolina Negroes, 1877–1900* (Columbia,
South Carolina, 1952); Vernon Lane Wharton, *The Negro in Mississippi, 1865–
1890* (Chapel Hill, North Carolina, 1947).

Bibliography

I. *Manuscripts*

Aside from the subject of politics, available and known manuscript collections are of little value to a study of this nature. Most of the white Virginians who left personal papers were lawyers and politicians, and they wrote about their vocation and avocation, and little else. Hence they are invaluable in the study of politics. (See Chapters I–IV.) And, for obvious reasons, aside from the Booker T. Washington Papers—a huge and difficult to use collection in the Library of Congress—there are no collections of Negro manuscripts of significant value. The Washington Papers are primarily concerned with Negro technical education, and most of the correspondence is through the Principal's Office of Tuskegee —valuable in itself but not to a study of this nature.

Curry, Jabez L. M. Library of Congress.
  Curry, as an agent of both the Peabody and Slater Funds, was a public education crusader. But as a Funder and a Conservative, he accepted the white Southern dictum that education for Negroes should be industrial and established the policy of the Peabody and Slater Funds of aiding only that type of Negro school. His papers include partisan and heated comments on Mahone and the Readjusters.

Daniel, John Warwick. Duke University Library.
  For a man of his importance in Virginia history, his personal papers are disappointing, consisting of largely Civil War reminiscenses by his friends; they contain a few letters from various Virginia politicians referring to Mahone, the debt question, and the Negro.

Eppes-Kilmartin Papers. University of Virginia Library.
  Papers of the south-central Virginia Eppes and Kilmartin families. Contain mostly political correspondence of a local nature in the Fourth Congressional District. Not always erudite, but forthright, honest, and of value.

Gregory Family Papers. University of Virginia Library.
  Papers of Captain James B. Gregory, including some political material. Letter from Governor William E. Cameron.

Hite, Cornelius Baldwin, Jr. Duke University Library.

Papers of the old Hite family of near Winchester in the Valley. Include letters of Cornelius H. Fauntleroy, student at the University of Virginia in 1883, to his grandmother, Mrs. Elizabeth A. Hite, with extremely interesting comments on the defeat of the Readjusters. A rare series in that they are critical of the Democrats. (Most Virginia manuscript material for this period is pro-Democratic and conservative.)

Jackson, Luther Porter. Virginia State College Library.

Papers of the late Negro historian. Clippings, routine correspondence, some of his notes, and Proceedings of the Negro Protective Association of Virginia. Unfortunately disappointing.

Kemper, James L. University of Virginia Library.

Although Kemper was Governor of Virginia, his papers contain little of real value—routine requests for political appointments while he was governor (1874–1878). After that the correspondence is mostly business and financial.

McCue Family Papers. University of Virginia Library.

Papers of a well-known Virginia family long active in the affairs of the central Piedmont and surrounding areas. Mostly legal and business papers, but also much material on late nineteenth-century politics, plus economic ventures in western Virginia.

Mahone, William A. Duke University Library.

A huge, invaluable collection, sorted but uncatalogued, containing a great deal of information on Mahone, the Readjusters, railroads, etc. Information on grass-roots politics from little known, local, political leaders, plus a large amount of correspondence from Harrison Holt Riddleberger. A "must" collection for any study of nineteenth-century Virginia after the Civil War.

Martin, Thomas Staples. James A. Bear, Jr., Collection of Political Papers of Martin. Charlottesville, Virginia.

A small but valuable collection of the papers of the Virginia machine boss, mostly in photostatic copies gathered from various sources, by the author of "Thomas Staples Martin: A Study in Virginia Politics, 1883–1896," Unpublished M. A. Thesis, University of Virginia, 1952.

O'Ferrall, Charles T. Executive Papers. Virginia State Library.
Like practically all the Executive Papers of Virginia's governors during this period, O'Ferrall's contain little of value by any standards. Outside of some interesting material on the activity of Coxe's Army while in the state, they largely concern requests for political appointments and hounding correspondence from some of O'Ferrall's creditors.

Tucker Family Papers. University of North Carolina Library.
Correspondence of John Randolph Tucker and his son H. St. George Tucker. The major portion consists of correspondence to the elder Tucker from his family. The only valuable letters are to H. St. George Tucker from such politicians as Camm Patteson and Edmund Randolph Cocke.

Woodall, John. Duke University Library.
Chiefly family correspondence, but this includes information on crops and economic conditions in general in Halifax and Prince Edward counties, with material on the condition of the small farmer from 1839–1870, and migration of both whites and Negroes to the West following the Civil War.

II. *Official Records*

Acts of the General Assembly of the State of Virginia.
Annual Reports (Virginia).
   (1) "Report[s] of the Board of Directors of the State Penitentiary."
   (2) *Report[s] of the Railroad Commissioner of the State of Virginia* (Bound and published separately as the *First Annual Report . . . Second Annual Report . . .* etc.
   (3) *School Report[s].*
Du Bois, W. E. B., "The Negroes of Farmville, Virginia: A Social Study," *Bulletin of the Department of Labor*, III (1898), 1–38.
Journal[s] of the House of Delegates of the State of Virginia.
Journal[s] of the Senate of the Commonwealth [State] of Virginia.
Report of the Proceedings and Debates of the Constitutional Convention, State of Virginia, 1901–1902, 2 vols.
United States Supreme Court Reports.
Virginia Code, 1873.
Virginia Constitution, 1902.

III. *Autobiographies and Memoirs*

Those cited here have the same virtues and weaknesses of all autobiographies and memoirs—presentatio: of motive and reactions amidst faded detail, colored memories, and a tendency to leave out all material unfavorable to the author. Valuable nonetheless, especially for revealing attitudes. (See Chapters VI and VII).

Barringer, Paul B., *The Natural Bent: The Memoirs of Dr. Paul B. Barringer*. Chapel Hill, N. C., 1949.

Butt, Rev. Israel L., *History of African Methodism in Virginia, or Four Decades in the Old Dominion*. Hampton, Va., 1908.

Claiborne, John Herbert, *Seventy-Five Years in Old Virginia*. New York, 1904.

Du Bois, W. E. B., *Dusk of Dawn: An Essay Toward an Autobiography of a Race Concept*. New York, 1940.

Goode, John, *Recollections of a Lifetime by John Goode of Virginia*. New York and Washington, D. C., 1906.

Hancock, Elizabeth H., editor, *Autobiography of John E. Massey*. New York and Washington, D. C., 1909.

McDonald, James J., *Life in Old Virginia*. Norfolk, Va., 1907.

Moton, Robert Russa, *Finding a Way Out: An Autobiography*. New York, 1920.

Munford, Beverly B., *Random Recollections*. New York, 1905.

Patteson, Camm, *The Young Bachelor*. Lynchburg, Va., 1900.

Watson, Walter A., *Notes on Southside Virginia*, edited by Mrs. Walter A. Watson, *Bulletin of the Virginia State Library*, XV (September, 1925).

Withers, Robert Enoch, *Autobiography of an Octogenarian*. Roanoke, Va., 1907.

IV.   *Travel Accounts*

Accounts of travelers are one of the richest sources of information for a study of this nature. Often they commented on things which had become so commonplace in the South that the natives were scarcely aware of their presence. Their naivetè was often disarming, and the white natives were as a result unusually frank with them. Comments of British travelers are interesting, in that their attitudes were so similar to those of native, white Virginians. But most interesting and valuable of all are the comments of French travelers, who were struck by the whole atmosphere of *inégalité*, and, unlike their more realistic and practical-minded English neighbors, immediately sought psychological and sociological reasons for it. And some of the explanations they offered were uncomfortably near the truth.

Anonymous, "A Social Study of Our Oldest Colony," *Littell's Living Age*, CLXI (1884), 168–175, 362–371.

Berry, C. B., *The Other Side: How it Struck Us*. London and New York, 1880.

Bryce, James, *The American Commonwealth*. 2 vols., New York and London, 1895, third edition.

Campbell, George, *White and Black; The Outcome of a Visit to the United States*. New York, 1879.

Clowes, W. Laird, *Black America: A Study of the Ex-Slave and his Late Master*. London, 1891.

Dixon, William Hepworth, *White Conquest*, 2 vols. London, 1876.

Freeman, Edward A., *Some Impressions of the United States*. New York, 1883.

Gaullieur, Henri, *Etudes Americaines*. Paris, 1891.

Harrison, J. B., "Studies in the South," *Atlantic Monthly*, L (1882), 99–110, 194–205, 349–361, 476–488, 623–633, 750–763.

Higginson, Thomas Wentworth, "Some War Scenes Revisited," *Atlantic Monthly*, XLII (July, 1878), 1–9.

Hole, Samuel Reynolds, *A Little Tour in America*. London and New York, 1895.

King, Edward, *The Great South*. Hartford, Conn., 1875.

Tricoche, George Nestler, *La Question Des Noirs Aux Etats-Unis*. Paris, 1894.

Saunders, William, *Through the Light Continent; Or The United States in 1877–8*. London, Paris, and New York, 1879.

Somers, Robert, *The Southern States Since the War, 1870–71*. London and New York, 1871.

See also Bonaparte, Evans James, "The Negro in the Writings of French and British Travelers to the United States, 1877–1900," below VII. UNPUBLISHED THESES, DISSERTATIONS, ETC.

V. *Other Primary Works*

Aptheker, Herbert, editor, *A Documentary History of the Negro People in the United States*. New York, 1951.

Bagby, George W., *The Old Virginia Gentleman and Other Sketches*, edited and arranged by Ellen M. Bagby. Richmond, Va., 1948 edition.

Barringer, Paul B., *The American Negro: His Past and Future*. Raleigh, N. C., 1900.

——— , *The Sacrifice of a Race*. Raleigh, N. C., 1900.

Blair, Lewis H., *The Prosperity of the South Dependent Upon the Elevation of the Negro*. Richmond, Va., 1889.

Bruce, Philip Alexander, *The Plantation Negro as a Freeman*. New York and London, 1889.

Cable, George W., *The Negro Question: A Selection of Writings in Civil Rights in the South*, edited by Arlin Turner. New York, 1958.
—— —, See below under VI. PRIMARY ARTICLES, for some of the above Cable selections as they originally appeared and as they are cited in the text here.
Groner, Virginius D., "Political Scrapbook," Hampton Institute. Newspaper clippings on the Negro from throughout the country.
Thomas, Alsen F., *The Virginia Constitutional Convention [of 1901–1902] and its Possibilities*. Lynchburg, Va., 1901.

VI. *Primary Articles*

The main virtue of this source is the fact that Northern periodicals furnished a publication outlet for white Southern liberals and educated, Southern Negroes. What Southern press there was, was conservative, and did not risk its already precarious position by publishing material critical of the South.

Armstrong, Samuel C., Frederick Douglas *et. al.*, "The Future of the Negro," *North American Review*, CXXXIX (July, 1884), 78–99.
Cable, George W., "A Simpler Negro Question," *Forum*, VI (December, 1888), 392–403.
—— —, "The Silent South," *Century Magazine*, XXX (September, 1875), 674–691.
—— —, "What Shall the Negro Do?" *Forum*, V (August, 1888), 627–639.
(Also see Cable above under V. OTHER PRIMARY WORKS.)
Davis, Noah, K., "The Negro in the New South," *Forum*, I (April, 1886), 126–135.
Editorial, "The Negro in the New South," *Outlook*, LXIII (October 7, 1899), 284–285.
—— —, "A Pathetic Appeal," *Outlook*, LXVIII (August 17, 1901), 903–904.
—— —, "Two Southern Views," *Outlook*, LXIX (November 30, 1901), 810–812.
Hampton, *Southern Workman*, 1872–1902. Published by the Hampton Institute. Scattered citations, signed and unsigned.
Price, J. C., "Does the Negro Seek Social Equality?" *Forum*, X (January, 1891), 558–564.
Riddleberger, Harrison H., "Bourbonism in Virginia," *North American Review*, CXXXIV (April, 1882), 416–430.
Ruffner, William H., "The Co-Education of the White and Colored Races," *Scribners Monthly*, VIII (1874), 86–90.

Bibliography

Stowe

Stowe, Harriet Beecher, "The Education of Freedman," (Part II), *North American Review*, CXXIX (July, 1879), 81–94. Also scattered material from *The Nation*.

VII. Unpublished Theses, Dissertations, etc.

Blackburn, Helen M., "The Populist Party in the South, 1890–1898," M. A. Thesis, Howard University, 1941.

Bonaparte, Evans James, "The Negro in the Writings of French and British travelers to the United States, 1877–1900," M. A. Thesis, Howard University, 1948. An able, well done, and valuable piece of work, particularly with reference to French travelers.

Bonner, Oscar Trent, "A Survey of Negro Education in Bedford County," M. A. Thesis, University of Virginia, 1939.

Crawford, George W., "John Mercer Langston—A Study in Virginia Politics, 1880–1890," M. A. Thesis, Virginia State College, 1940.

Eckenrode, Hamilton James, "History of Virginia Since 1865; 1865–1945; A Political History," University of Virginia Library. This is perhaps the ablest work of all Eckenrode's productions; certainly it is the most liberal. Eminently fair to Mahone.

Horn, Herman L., "The growth and Development of the Democratic Party in Virginia Since 1890," Ph.D. Dissertation, Duke University, 1949. Microfilm copy in University of Virginia Library. This is one of the ablest works of a broad scope done on Virginia politics in many years.

Lloyd, Hermione Elizabeth, "History of the Public Education of the Negro in Virginia," M. A. Thesis, Howard University, 1936.

McFarland, George M., "Extension of Democracy in Virginia, 1850–1895," Ph.D. Dissertation, Princeton University, 1934. Microfilm copy in University of Virginia Library.

Walton, Thomas Eugene, "The Negro in Richmond, 1880–1890," M. A. Thesis, Howard University, 1950. Many more narrow-in-time and thorough-in-coverage studies of this nature must be done before a definitive history of the Negro in Virginia can ever be written.

VIII. Newspapers

(All are Virginia newspapers unless otherwise specified. Negro newspapers are identified.)

The student cannot afford to omit the use of newspapers, but both he and the reader need to remember that where the Negro was concerned in post-1865 Virginia, the newspapers were written more to justify and persuade than they were to inform.

Covington, *Alleghany Tribune*.
Harrisonburg, *Old Commonwealth*.
———, *Rockingham Register*.
Lynchburg, *Daily Advance*.
New Market, *Shenandoah Valley*.
Petersburg, *Lancet* (Negro).
Richmond, *Daily Dispatch* (or *Dispatch*).
Richmond, *Enquirer*.
———, *Planet* (Negro).
———, *State*.
———, *Times* (or *Twice A Week Times*).
———, *Virginia Star* (Negro).
———, *Virginia Sun* (Populist).
———, *Weekly Dispatch*.
———, *Whig* (or *Weekly Whig*).
Staunton, *Spectator*.
Washington, D. C., *Bee* (Negro).

IX.   *Secondary Works*

Appleton's Annual Cyclopedia.
Blake, Nelson M., *William Mahone of Virginia: Soldier and Political Insurgent*. Richmond, Va., 1935.
Brenaman, Jacob A., *A History of Virginia Conventions*. Richmond Va., 1902.
Brown, William Henry, *The Education and Economic Development of the Negro in Virginia* (Phelps-Stokes Fellowship Paper of the University of Virginia). Charlottesville, Va., 1923.
Bruce, Philip Alexander, *The Rise of the New South* (vol. XVII of *The History of North America*). Philadelphia, Pa., 1905.
Gray, Lewis Cecil, *Southern Agriculture, Plantation System, and the Negro Problem*. Philadelphia, Pa., (?), n. d.
Green, Fletcher M., "Some Aspects of the Convict Lease System in the Southern States," *Essays in Southern History*, edited by Fletcher M. Green (vol. XXXI of *The James Sprunt Studies in History and Political Science*). Chapel Hill, N. C., 1949, pp. 112–123.
Harlan, Louis R., *Separate and Unequal: Public School Campaigns and Racism in the Southern Seaboard States, 1901–1915*. Chapel Hill, N. C., 1958.
Ingle, Edward, "The Negro in the District of Columbia," *Johns Hopkins University Studies in Historical and Political Science*, XI (1893), 7–110.

Jackson, Luther P., *Negro Office-Holders in Virginia, 1865–1895.* Norfolk, Va., 1945.

Johnson, Charles A., *A Narrative History of Wise County, Virginia.* Kingsport, Tenn., 1938.

Johnson, Guion G., "The Idealogy of White Supremacy," *Essays in Southern History,* edited by Fletcher M. Green (vol. XXXI of *The James Sprunt Studies in History and Political Science*). Chapel Hill, N. C., 1949, pp. 124–156.

LeConte, Joseph, *The Race Problem in the South* in *Man and the State* —*Studies in Applied Sociology.* New York, 1892.

Lewinson, Paul, *Race, Class, & Party: A History of Negro Suffrage and White Politics in the South.* New York, 1932.

McDanel, Ralph Clipman, "The Virginia Constitutional Convention of 1901–1902," *Johns Hopkins University Studies in Historical and Political Science,* XLVI (1928), 243–406. Outdated, but it will remain valuable until a new and more thorough study is done.

Martin, Robert E., "Negro Disfranchisement in Virginia," *Howard University Studies in the Social Sciences,* I (1938).

Moger, Allen Wesley, *The Rebuilding of the Old Dominion: A Study in Economic, Social, and Political Transition from 1880 to 1902.* Ann Arbor, Mich., 1940.

Morton, Richard L., *The Negro in Virginia Politics, 1865–1902.* Charlottesville, Va., 1919. Outdated but still valuable.

Pearson, Charles C., *The Readjuster Movement in Virginia.* New Haven, Conn., and London, 1917.

Pendleton, William C., *Political History of Appalachian Virginia, 1776–1927.* Dayton, Va., 1927. Not always the best of scholarship, but a significant aid in balancing out the better known eastern story.

Pinchbeck, Raymond B., *The Virginia Negro Artisan and Tradesman.* (Phelps-Stokes Fellowship Paper of the University of Virginia). Richmond, Va., 1926.

Porter, Albert O., *County Government in Virginia: A Legislative History, 1607–1904* (No. 506 of *Columbia University Studies in History, Economics, and Public Law*). New York, 1947.

Pulliam, David L., *The Constitutional Conventions of Virginia from the Foundation of the Commonwealth to the Present Time.* Richmond, Va., 1901.

Sheldon, William DuBose, *Populism in the Old Dominion: Virginia Farm Politics, 1885–1900.* Princeton, N. J., 1935. Still essentially sound after more than twenty-five years.

Smith, Samuel Denny, *The Negro in Congress, 1870–1901.* Chapel Hill, N. C., 1940.

Snavely, Tipton Ray, *The Taxation of Negroes in Virginia* (Phelps-Stokes Fellowship Paper of the University of Virginia). Charlottesville, Va., 1916.

Squires, W. H. T., *Land of Decision.* Portsmouth, Va., 1931.

Stephenson, Gilbert Thomas, *Race Distinctions in American Law.* New York, 1910.

Taylor, Alrutheus A., *The Negro in the Reconstruction of Virginia.* Washington, D. C., 1926. Appeared earlier in the *Journal of Negro History,* XI (April and July 1926), 243–415, 425–537. Still a good guide or blueprint to the study of the role of the Negro in the Virginia of 1865–1880. As most phases of Negro life are treated, it serves as a good point of investigative departure.

Warrock Richardson Almanack, Richmond, Virginia.

Wayland, John W., *Historic Harrisonburg.* Staunton, Va., 1949.

———, *A History of Rockingham County.* Dayton, Va., 1912.

Woodward, C. Vann, *Origins of the New South, 1877–1913* (vol. IX of *A History of the South,* edited by Wendell Holmes Stephenson and E. Merton Coulter, 10 vols., Louisiana State University, 1947———). Louisiana State University, 1951.

———, *The Strange Career of Jim Crow.* New York, 1957, revised edition. Provocative and suggestive work which prompted this whole study.

Work Projects Administration, Writers Program, *The Negro in Virginia.* New York, 1940.

X. *Secondary Articles*

Franklin, John Hope, "History of Racial Segregation in the United States," *Annals of the American Academy of Political and Social Science,* CCCIV (March, 1956), 1–9.

Johnston, James Hugo, "The Participation of Negroes in the Government of Virginia from 1877 to 1888," *Journal of Negro History,* XIV (July, 1929), 251–271.

Murphy, L. E., "The Civil Rights Law of 1875," *Journal of Negro History,* XII (April, 1927), 110–127.

Taylor, Alrutheus A., "The Negro in the Reconstruction of Virginia," *Journal of Negro History,* XI (April and July, 1926), 243–415, 425–537. See above, under IX. SECONDARY WORKS.

Weatherford, W. D., "Race Relationship in the South," *Annals of the American Academy of Political and Social Science,* XLIX (1913), 164–172.

Wynes, Charles E., "Charles T. O'Ferrall and the Virginia Gubernatorial Election of 1893," *Virginia Magazine of History and Biography,* XLIV (October, 1956), 437–453.

Index

Index 163